THE
LENTEN
LABYRINTH

THE
LENTEN LABYRINTH

DAILY REFLECTIONS
FOR THE JOURNEY OF LENT

EDWARD HAYS

Forest of Peace
P u b l i s h i n g

Suppliers for the Spiritual Pilgrim

Other Books by the Author:
(available from the publisher)

Prayers and Rituals
Prayers for a Planetary Pilgrim
Prayers for the Domestic Church
Prayers for the Servants of God

Contemporary Spirituality
Feathers on the Wind
Holy Fools & Mad Hatters
A Pilgrim's Almanac
Pray All Ways
Secular Sanctity
In Pursuit of the Great White Rabbit
The Ascent of the Mountain of God

Parables and Stories
The Quest for the Flaming Pearl
St. George and the Dragon
The Magic Lantern
The Ethiopian Tattoo Shop
Twelve and One-Half Keys
Sundancer
The Christmas Eve Storyteller

The Lenten Labyrinth

copyright © 1994, by Edward M. Hays

Library of Congress Catalog Card Number: 93-74707
ISBN: 0-939516-22-5

published by
Forest of Peace Publishing, Inc.
PO Box 269
Leavenworth, KS 66048-0269   USA

printed by
Hall Directory, Inc.
Topeka, KS 66608-0348

1st printing: January 1994
2nd printing: January 1995
3rd printing: January 1996

Dedicated to

Thomas Melchior
a faithful friend

CONTENTS

INTRODUCTION

Rejoice! You are about to begin a great adventure and a journey of transformation which holds the power to change—to radically enrich—your way of thinking, loving and believing. Know that as you prepare to make the first step on this journey, you are doing so in the company of many other pilgrims. While it will be a private—or rather a *personal*—retreat and renewal, at the same time it will be a global venture, shared with your brother and sister Christians.

Rejoice also in the companionship of the Communion of Saints. Not only do you walk in faith with others around the world today, you are accompanied in your pursuit of holiness by the holy ones of previous ages. They sound the ancient trumpet call to begin the work of Lent: "Remember you are dust." It rings loud and clear: "Remember how short is life, how close is your death, so do not delay." Make each of the forty days and nights significant. Let this be an occasion to act like the saints instead of simply dreaming about how you would like to act.

Rejoice each time you have the opportunity to perform a hidden act of prayer, penance or charity. Jesus promised that God, with whom there are no secrets, will respond to your every deed with generous affection.

Rejoice too that God's Spirit is your Lenten companion. Just as the Spirit of the Holy led Jesus into his Lenten desert of forty days, that same Spirit is leading you. Walk with confidence, but be aware that there are many steps on the way. Today, as you begin your Lenten journey, you may feel strong of heart, filled with a desire for renewal and a thirst for holiness. Be prepared, however, that as the Lenten days grow in number you may lose your enthusiasm to be a saint and may lust to return to your old ways. Yet rejoice and be glad, for God's Spirit will, if you ask, lead you gently back to the path of reform and inspire you to even greater zeal.

Rejoice in the victory of those who complete the course of this journey of reform. Face with honesty your fear of the cross, of the pain that it holds, and the ugliness of Calvary. Then look beyond these to the victory of the empty tomb, the sunrise alleluias of Easter.

Rejoice that, in the wisdom of God, you are invited to take up your cross, as Jesus embraced his, and to follow our Master as you deny your very self. Rejoice in that dignity of being a co-redeemer of the world. As you are reconciled to others, as your heart becomes more peaceful, more filled with God, so does all the earth.

Come, friend, it is time to approach the gates of the Lenten labyrinth. It is time, with courage and grace, to open those gates and to enter into that great mystery of renewal, death and resurrection.

ASH WEDNESDAY

Today your home should be decorated in Halloween fashion as you stand at the gateway to the great Lenten labyrinth. Before swinging open the iron gate of the labyrinth, ponder these lines of Edna St. Vincent Millay's poem, "Dirge without Music."

> Down, down, down into the darkness of the grave
> Gently they go, the beautiful, the tender, the kind;
> Quietly they go, the intelligent, the witty, the brave.
> I know. But I do not approve. And I am not resigned.

Among all the animals, humans are the only ones we know of who can ponder their own death. Yet while all humans can, few do. We prefer to be like our cats or dogs and think only of today or our next meal.

Ash Wednesday challenges us to ponder the reality we most dread to consider: our own death. The journey of the labyrinth and the way of the disciple of Christ begins with the task of seriously reflecting on one's own death, embracing it so that one can truly embrace life.

May the gift of holy ashes placed on your forehead on this ancient holy day (or a plastic packet of dust or earth you prepare*) help you to realize that only by a Christlike death can you experience the promise of Easter's life.

Some dust of the earth in a small plastic bag can be a useful Lenten aid. Place it in your prayer corner or on your desk as a daily reminder of death. It will help you treat each of these forty days as significant.

ASH THURSDAY

Today the iron gate of the Lenten labyrinth swings open. The creaking sound of its hinges can make you aware that before you lies a long journey of forty days and nights. Before crossing the threshold, take time to consider well the serious consequences of such a Lenten adventure.

Recall the ashes of yesterday (or hold in your hand the plastic bag of earth you have prepared), and consider your death. Such a labyrinth reflection can be frightening. You and I can easily echo those lines of the poem, "I do not approve (of death). And I am not resigned (to my own death or the death of those I love)."

The journey of this Lent involves following in the footsteps of Christ. It is not like acting in some Passion Play, but is a real experience of the cross in real life. Right in the midst of daily life, we can walk the road up to

Calvary and down to the tomb—so as to taste the joy of sunrise on Easter Sunday.

On this Ash Thursday, could you or I embrace death? Could we die at peace, reconciled with those with whom we live and work? To the extent we are not resigned to the reality of dying, let our Ash Thursday prayer be:

> O God, come to my assistance.
> Help me embrace my death at the hour
>   and in the manner you deem best for me,
>   even if it involves pain, disgrace
>   or absolute aloneness.
> By such acceptance of your will,
>   may I share with Christ
>   in the redemption of the world.

ASH OR MARDI FRIDAY

In some traditions the Tuesday before Ash Wednesday is called *Mardi Gras* or Fat Tuesday and is a time for celebration and carnival. The Friday after Ash Wednesday is also a carnival time for masks and merrymaking.

Today, as you take your first step across the Lenten threshold, you should do so with a smile! While the steps that lead upward from the Ash Wednesday vestibule to the complicated labyrinth are littered with skulls, bones and other signs of death, you can enter this solemn season smiling. Remember Jesus' instructions to his disciples

12

when they wanted to fast and do penance. Not only were they to do so in secret, they were to have bright and cheerful faces.

Mardi Friday is Mirror Friday. It is a day to see if you are wearing the sad face of gloom and doom so that you will look like a serious Lenten pilgrim. While you are called to pick up your cross and follow after Jesus, called to embrace the serious work of reform and renewal, you are to do so with a joyful spirit and a smile.

What kind of face or mask are you wearing on this first Friday in Lent? Perhaps you might best be faithful to the wishes of Jesus by putting on a Mardi Gras clown's mask today while you die to yourself so as to live in Christ.

ASH OR SACKCLOTH SATURDAY

Having climbed the three holy steps that lead up from Lent's entrance gate, you will find a rack of garments. They are unique wedding garments made of sackcloth, and all the guests at this feast of fasting and penance are expected to wear one.

Before you choose one, know that they're not comfortable, but they are the proper attire for anyone traveling the Lenten labyrinth. The clue to their importance is not so much the material—although sackcloth is the ancient sign of penance—it is rather in the two pockets that are small sacks sewn into the garment. Don't leave home to travel the maze of these forty days without a sackful of hope and a sackful of faith.

Look down and you will see carved in the pavement at the entrance to the labyrinth the words "Abandon all despair, you who enter here." Do not reflect upon your death with a sense of despair, saying to yourself, "Eat, drink and be merry, for tomorrow I shall die." Rather, aware that your right pocket is full of hope, say, "Eat, drink and be merry (*or* fast and be merry), since, by the process of Lenten reform, I shall not die but live!"

Pray on this Sackcloth Saturday not to be scared to death by death but to be scared to life by reflecting on how brief and fleeting is the happiness of life. Put on your sackcloth garment with its pocketful of faith and take some time to reflect on what aspects of your life need to be reformed and redesigned. Have faith that God will grace you with whatever you need to truly change your life.

Pledge yourself on this vigil of the first Sunday of Lent to embrace whatever penance is required for that reform to be achieved. Pledge yourself to embrace the pain of that penance not as a forty day reform but as a permanent life change. Let the sackcloth bookmark that came with this volume help you keep the "feel" of Lent throughout the forty days of this labyrinthian journey.

FIRST SUNDAY IN LENT

Once again God calls you, and all of us, to greatness as another Lent begins. God calls you, as God called the whole Israelite community, to rise up to the greatest challenge ever given to humanity—the challenge to be God-like. In the book of Leviticus we hear that God said to Moses, "Speak to the whole Israelite community and tell them: Be holy, for I, your God, am holy" (Lv. 19: 1-2).

Jesus echoed that call to be holy, God-like, challenging his disciples to a lifelong Lent, in the account of Matthew,

> You have heard the commandment, "An eye for an eye, a tooth for a tooth." But what I say to you is: offer no resistance to injury. When a person strikes you on the right cheek, turn and offer the other. If anyone wants to go to law over your shirt, hand over your coat as well. Should anyone press you into service for one mile, go two miles. Give to the one who begs from you, and do not turn your back on the borrower.

You have heard the commandment, "You shall love those of your own country but hate your enemy." My command to you is: "Love your enemies, pray for your persecutors" (Mt. 5: 38-44).

To achieve that ability to love friends and enemies alike, to respond with kindness rather than revenge, requires a journey away from old ways into new ways of responding. Those ways are mirrored in the labyrinth design shown at the beginning of this Sunday reflection.

This design could be a new pattern for Lenten worship folders and parish missalettes. Instead of prayers and artwork on the covers, why not crossword puzzles or puzzles in which you have to find your way to the center? When worshipers arrive at church early to get a good seat, these puzzles would give them something to occupy their time. A good crossword puzzle would be excellent entertainment during a dull sermon or one of those long solos by musicians who seem to be more in love with their own voices than they are with God.

The puzzle pictured is about 800 years old. The original labyrinth pattern, about forty feet wide, is on the stone floor of the Cathedral of Notre Dame at Chartres in France. We know that Chartres was no fun-and-games center, so what was the purpose of putting a puzzle in the middle of a cathedral? Chartres was one of the great sites of medieval pilgrimages. Like most of the cathedrals of Europe, it was also a great catechism. The stained glass windows, the marvel of the cathedral, contain over one thousand images of biblical stories, scenes of parables and saints—not to mention all the saints and images in the statuary and stone carvings. The cathedral was a giant technicolor theological textbook, and the labyrinth-puzzle on the floor was perhaps the most important lesson for pilgrims who journeyed there. It provided an experiential teaching about the journey of life.

Labyrinths are over 4,000 years old. The original ones appeared in the middle of the third century B.C. in Egypt. Some of them were below ground and some above ground. Later labyrinths have taken on a variety of forms. Among the most common are walled gardens with tall hedges shaped in the form of a maze. Others are intricate passageways such as the one in the Chartres Cathedral.

The complex twisting patterns of a maze have many loops. They take one back and forth, almost retracing the same path. There are blind alleys, dead ends and few shortcuts. Nearly all labyrinths were intended to be maze-maps reflecting each person's journey to God.

As Lent begins, you need to ask yourself where you are on this ancient map. As you find your place, whether at the beginning of the labyrinth, in the middle or near the end, you can ask another question: "Where am I going?" That's a popular question today. The paradox at the dawn of a new millennium is that anyone who knows where he or she is going probably really isn't going anywhere!

Social structures and institutions are changing so rapidly that no one knows how the way will unfold. If you are honest, you know that life is indeed like a tall walled maze. Contrary to what you might have been taught, the journey to God today is not some long linear path, but more like a complicated labyrinth.

❊   ❊   ❊

Ask yourself on this Lenten Sunday: "Where am I going?"
Do you feel fearful if you do not know the answer? Or do you
feel confident that if you are seeking the Reign of God with all
your heart you have nothing to fear since God will provide all
you need? This great Lenten journey will hopefully teach you
such a calm assurance as you walk a pathway in which you
often can see no further than a day or so ahead.

❀　　❀　　❀

FIRST MONDAY IN LENT

In both the labyrinths of Lent and life, with their puzzling
pathways, you logically may ask, "Am I provided with
some guides for this journey?" Yes, you are. One of them
is Moses who is given to you as an excellent labyrinthian
standard bearer. He relayed God's message to the People
of God wandering in the desert:

> You shall not bear hatred for your neighbor in
> your heart. Though you may have cause to
> reprove your neighbor, do not incur sin because
> of him or her. Take no revenge and cherish no
> grudge against those of your own country. You
> shall love your neighbor as yourself. I am your
> God (Lv. 19: 17).

Do not hate. Do not follow the pathways of hate, for
you will never make it to the center of the labyrinth. Do

not nurse a grudge in your heart because if you nurse grudges you're not going to find the way. Likewise, do not seek revenge.

Moses told us not to do what comes naturally, not to follow the "natural" *low road* of our primal nature. That lower nature urges us to strike back when someone strikes out in anger. Moses told us to take the *high road*, to respond to the higher nature within us. Only by following that higher call can we find the way home. No matter how complex your journey, how twisting and turning back upon itself the road may seem, as long as you seek God with all your heart, you will find your way to the mystical rose at the center of the labyrinth.

❀　❀　❀

Reflect today on which of the two roads—or alternating from one to the other—you habitually travel. How do you detour from the low road to reach the high road when you are caught up in a strong emotion?

❀　❀　❀

FIRST TUESDAY IN LENT

While seeking God with all your heart and possessing a calm assurance provides a compass for those on life's labyrinthian road, being relaxed and confident isn't easy.

You and I know from experience that fear and doubt are companion pilgrims on such a pathway. Rather than a feeling of being safely on the way home, we're more likely to be puzzled because of feeling lost.

Did I make the right turn? Did I do the right thing? Some people who are lost in the dark encourage themselves by whistling when they're afraid. Pilgrims of the labyrinth who feel lost in the maze are less likely to whistle than to sing the classic song "Amazing Grace."

Amazing grace has banished fear
And given life to me.
I once was lost but now am found,
Was blind but now I see.

What is it that I see? The amazing grace is how I see that if I am a*mazed*, if I am in the maze, then I'm already inside the rose at the heart of the labyrinth. I see that each of the loops of the passageway is just an outer petal. Anyone who is on the way is already *in* the way. The fourteenth century mystic St. Catherine of Siena said, "All the way to God *is* God." Christ said, "I am the Way."

❀　　❀　　❀

Reflect on the subject of eyesight today. What do you see when you look at your life? Do you see it as some detour that you are forced to take because of circumstances or events beyond your control? Do you see it not only as a way to God but as a moment by moment communion with God? Are you blind or a sighted person?

❀　　❀　　❀

FIRST WEDNESDAY IN LENT

All the way to God is *gulistan*. Among Islamic mystics *gulistan* is the name for paradise, and *gulistan* is a rose garden. We are simply weaving our way around the petals of the rose. That is the wonderful good news of the great catechism of Chartres.

For pilgrims in medieval Europe there was one great unbreakable vow: to make a pilgrimage to Jerusalem. Of course, during the time of the Great Crusades that was impossible. So the church designated seven great cathedrals. One could fulfill the great vow by making a pilgrimage to one of these sacred spots. When pilgrims to Chartres arrived at their destination, they found a puzzle. But the puzzle was inside the cathedral. That fact itself was part of the lesson. Even as the pilgrims walked the mystic pattern, they were inside that which they sought. The same is true for you.

St. Paul in his First Letter to the Corinthians said, "You are the temple of God" (1 Cor. 3: 18). We are living stones, all of us together. We are the temple. We are what we seek. So, rejoice! There is nowhere to go; there is nothing to learn. You need only to see! Yet that seems like foolishness. So Paul says, "Well, you had better become a fool!"(1 Cor. 3: 18). It's hard to be a fool though. It's hard not to want to be in control.

Good advice for anyone walking the maze is found in an old Russian fairy tale. It says, "Go, not knowing where! Take, not knowing what! The path is long, the way is unknown and the hero does not know how to reach the end by himself or herself." You can't take anything along—no provisions? Well, the secret lies in eating the map! It is the journey itself that is the nourishment. Once you know—are *amazed*—that what you're doing at this moment—traveling that complicated pathway which leads to God—is *amazing*, suddenly everything has meaning.

There is a story from the Middle Ages:

A person came to one of the great cathedrals that was being built and stopped at three stone masons who were carving away. The pilgrim asked them all the same question: "What are you doing?"

The first mason said, "Chipping stone, as you can see." The second mason said, "I am making a living. I'm providing food and shelter for my family." And the third mason said, "I am building a great cathedral!"

People who know where they are possess those jewelers' glasses which are able to magnify the most insignificant events of life so that they become very significant. Every twist and turn has purpose, especially when you remember the first and great commandment of God: "Be holy, for I your God am holy." It's not difficult to be holy, for we were made in the image of the Holy. It doesn't call for some complicated Spiritual Doctor's degree. Just act naturally today according to your higher nature.

❀   ❀   ❀

How do you view your life's work: as part of the building up of a great cathedral—the church, the Body of Christ—or simply as a means to making a living? An important Lenten work is learning to see whatever work you do as being part of the great and divine design to re-create the world.

❀   ❀   ❀

FIRST THURSDAY IN LENT

Traveling the maze of the way is the greatest of all adventures. It is the only adventure that gets better the older you are! Unlike basketball or gymnastics or sailing, it has nothing to do with youthful physical agility—or wealth! It is the greatest adventure. And those who are *amazed* are joyful because they know that that's why they're here on earth—to be *amazed*.

They also know that the closer you get to the center, the happier you become. People who are unhappy in life are usually those who feel lost and confused. They're unhappy, first of all, because they don't know they're in the midst of the mystical maze and keep looking for the path somewhere else.

Another reason for their unhappiness is that they live on the outer rim of the labyrinth. Instead of being pilgrims of the path, they've camped out on the periphery and are no longer seekers of the rose at the center. The secret of happiness lies in the awareness that the closer you come to the center, the happier you become.

Sprinkled throughout the Old Testament are over

eighty beatitudes. The beatitudes of the maze provide a threefold introduction to Lent:

> Blessed are the *amazed*, for they shall need God—
> and the needy shall become saints.
> Blessed are the puzzled, for they shall become
> prayerful.
> Blessed further are the prayerful, for they shall live
> in perpetual communion with God.

Jesus is also given to you as a guide. The good news is his travelers' information. Jesus says, "As you walk down the pathway and you see a sign that reads, 'An eye for an eye—if someone hurts you, hurt 'em back,' don't go that way. It's a dead end. Returning violence for violence is literally a dead end. If you see a sign that says, 'Don't feel obligated,' don't go that way. *Be* obligated. Be generous. Be luxurious in your love. That's the way to the rose at the center. When you see a sign in the maze that says, 'Love those of your own country, love your neighbors but hate your enemies,' do not go that way either, for that law will never take you all the way home."

Jesus was being naughty when he said that was the old law, for no place in the First Testament does it say you are to love your neighbor and hate your enemy. What he was saying is, "You've all made yourselves scholars at interpreting the law. The law says, 'Love your neighbor as yourself,' and you interpreted it as, 'Only Jews are our neighbors. Therefore, we must love those who are Jewish, but we can hate the Samaritan.'"

You and I are like them; we interpret God's law today. We have so often said, "Love Americans, but hate *them*"—whoever "them" happens to be at the moment. Jesus said, "No, I want to make it very clear that the sign that leads to the center of the way says, 'Love your neighbor *and* love your enemies.'" Follow that pathway and you will circle closer and closer to the rose.

❀　　❀　　❀

Reflect today on whether you have twisted and turned God's law of love to serve your own purposes. People are people and it is not unusual to see others as difficult. It is easy to see and treat others as enemies because of how they treat you. Make your prayer this Lenten day a prayer of blessing toward those whom you feel misunderstand, dislike or even hate you.

Praying for those who have injured you, truly asking God to bless them, is an excellent Lenten act of self-denial.

❀　　❀　　❀

FIRST FRIDAY IN LENT

The Lenten labyrinth is full of twists and turns and dead ends because it patterns in forty days the road of life. If you look closely at the design of the labyrinth from Chartres, you will see that there is one turn for each of the forty days—four quadrants of ten paths each—before one reaches the inner circle of Holy Week. It is a pattern that mirrors life.

Usually when we come to one of life's blank walls or

dead ends, the frustration of failure drains the sap out of us. We can easily sink to our knees and give up. In the words of that old song:

> Through many dangers, toils and snares
> I have already come.
> It's grace that's brought me safe thus far
> And grace will lead me home.

That's wonderful news: "And grace will lead me home." It's the grace to create space in your life to listen. It's the grace to stand seemingly lost in the maze, not sure where you are, and yet to know that if you listen, you'll hear God calling you by name: "Robert, this way." "Kathleen, come this way."

"Grace will lead you home"—if you but listen and are foolish enough not to trust solely in your intellect. Rejoice, as this first week of Lent draws to a close, in that amazing grace, for all you have to do is let grace bring you home. Rejoice! Take up the Lenten journey not with that gloom and doom of the old Lent. Why should you enter into this season with a heavy soul? It's a great adventure!

Sadly, so many Christians—while it's an adventure like climbing Mt. Everest—begin Lent to the strains of "The Volga Boatman." That's not the melody of this journey. Rejoice, even if you feel you're at a dead end or in some blind alley. Rejoice, no matter how many mistakes you've made in life, no matter how many "F's" you've gotten for the previous ways you've traveled this ancient pathway. Every "F" is a lesson, and you have only to learn from life's lessons.

❀　　❀　　❀

Consider today how the old traditions of Lent, perhaps reinforced by purple banners and old rugged crosses, may influence your way of living these days. Is the purpose of Lent penance and self-denial, or is it reform, reconstruction and renewal? While remodeling your home can be painful and difficult, it is not an occasion for remorse and gloom. Neither is Lent.

❋   ❋   ❋

FIRST SATURDAY IN LENT

As we prepare to conclude the first week of Lent, we reflect on the kind of equipment needed for the Lenten journey in the labyrinth. While the old Russian fairy tale advised taking along no provisions, I would propose three traveling aids for those who want to walk the labyrinth.

The first is a sense of flexibility so that when you come to a dead end you can turn around and find a new direction rather than sitting down to weep and wail. Along with flexibility, creativity and humor are essential for anyone in the maze. Each of these provisions for the way is addressed in a parable to ponder:

Once there was a Jewish rabbi who had a servant named Jacob. They would often ride together in a horse-drawn cart. The rabbi was extremely fond of his wonderful horse. It was a beautiful, brown, lively animal. Once, when they were traveling through Russia, the rabbi decided to spend the night at an inn in a small town. As was the custom, Jacob, the servant, spent the night at the stable with the horse.

Into the stable that night came a horse trader with a big bottle of vodka. He made friends with Jacob, and they drank and drank until the early hours of the morning, when the horse trader bought the rabbi's horse for a song. The next morning the servant woke up horrified at what he had done. He didn't know what to do next, for at any moment the rabbi would arrive. So he ran over, picked up the cart, placed himself between the cart poles and began munching on the straw.

The rabbi came out of the inn and said, "What is this? Where is my horse?"

Jacob said, "Horse? I'm your horse!"

The rabbi said, "You must be insane! Jacob, have you lost your mind? What has happened to my horse?"

Jacob responded, "Rabbi, don't get angry. I must make a confession to you. Many years ago, I failed. I slipped and fell. I had sex with a woman who wasn't my wife. What's really bad, Rabbi, is that I enjoyed it and I wasn't sorry. God punished me by making me a horse—your horse! For all these years I've pulled your cart around, and today my penance is over! Blessed be God!"

The poor rabbi who was devout said, "Well, all things are possible with God. This is amazing!" While the rabbi was swept off his feet by this miraculous event, there was a practical problem. How could they continue their journey without a horse?

So the rabbi had Jacob wait there and went to the market. When he came to the horse traders, he found himself face to face with his own horse who was munching on some hay. He went up and whispered in the horse's ear, "Goodness sake, Jacob, so soon again?"

❀　　❀　　❀

This parable of humor and creativity can set your Lenten course with good laughter and a sense of freedom as you complete the adventure of this first week of Lent.

Prayerfully reflect now on the Lenten call to both foolishness and profound dignity since God's Spirit is within you. Read and ponder carefully these words from the First Letter of Paul to the Corinthians:

> *Are you not aware that you are the temple of God and that the Spirit of God dwells within you? If anyone destroys God's temple, God will destroy that one. For the temple of God is holy, and you are that temple.*
>
> *Let none of you delude yourselves. If any of you think yourselves wise in a worldly way, you had better become fools. In that way you will really be wise for the wisdom of this world is absurdity with God (1 Cor. 3: 16-19).*

❀　　❀　　❀

SECOND SUNDAY IN LENT

The Gospel of Matthew provides a preview of coming attractions, particularly the coming attraction of Easter Sunday and our personal resurrections from the tomb.

Jesus took Peter, James and John and led them up on a high mountain by themselves and was transfigured before their eyes. His face became as dazzling as the sun and his clothes as radiant as light. Suddenly Moses and Elijah appeared visiting with Jesus. Peter cried out, "Lord, how good it is for us to be here! With your permission I will erect three booths here, one for you, one for Moses and one for Elijah." While he was speaking, suddenly a bright cloud overshadowed them, and a voice said, "This is my beloved Son upon whom my favor rests. Listen to him." The disciples fell to the ground, overcome with fear. Jesus laid his hand upon them, and said, "Get up! Do not be afraid." When they looked up, they did not see anyone but Jesus, and he commanded them, "Do not tell anyone of this until the Son of Man rises from the dead" (Mt. 17: 1-9).

Today you turn into another path of the labyrinth. As you do, you're given a trailblazer, a wonderful guide, Old Abraham. Recall his story from the book of Genesis:

> God said to Abram, "Go forth from the land of your kinsfolk and from your parents' house to a land that I will show you. I will make of you a great nation, and I will bless you." Abram went as God directed him. Abram was seventy-five years old when he left Haran (Gen. 12: 1-2,4).

Abraham could relate well to the instructions given in the Russian fairy tale: "Go, not knowing where! Take, not knowing what! The way is unknown, the path is long. Even the hero does not know how to reach the end by himself or herself."

That's a perfect description of the instructions given to Abraham and Sarah. They were told by God simply to "Go!" God never told them *where* to go, just, "Go, be on your way." It's a marvelous story, and so unlike what you and I would like to hear. It's difficult to consider leaving home without having a definite destination. Who would even go off on a brief holiday, let alone leave home, family and profession, to go someplace unknown? Adolescents and young people more easily handle such ambiguous travel. Out of a sense of adventure they take off to spend the summer in Europe with only a vague idea of where they will travel or stay. They're even inclined to take trips with LSD or drugs, not knowing where such "trips" will lead them. As mature adults we seldom leave home without a thorough road map of where we are bound.

The good news is that Abraham was seventy-five years old—part of the geriatrics generation. Countless are those who aren't even close to the geriatrics generation yet spend their lives in rocking chairs. If you are one of them, what's going to get you out of your rocking chair and into the adventure of life? What will pry you from the security of your daily routine or unglue your feet from home plate? Perhaps a good slogan or motto would help.

An excellent motto for any Lenten labyrinth traveler is the one found on an American railroad logo. It's perfect for Lent even if you've never related it to this season of reform. It appears on boxcars, passenger cars, diesel engines and calendars, and it sums up what's needed for your labyrinth journey. The perfect Lenten logo is a blue cross on a white circular field, on which are the words *Santa Fe.*

It's the name of the railroad that became famous for its route from Atchison, Kansas through Topeka to the city of Santa Fe, New Mexico. The slogan of the railroad is, "Santa Fe, All the Way." Santa Fe is actually an abridged name for the city founded in 1610 by the Spanish, *Villa real de la Santa Fe de la San Francisco*, "the Royal City of the Holy Faith of St. Francis (of Assisi)." The short form is simply *Santa Fe*, "Holy Faith."

❦   ❦   ❦

The directions for walking the Lenten maze are equally simple, "Holy Faith, All the Way." Reflect on this second Sunday of Lent if you are walking the way of life with a holy faith. While most of us place faith in various machines, insurance companies and a variety of institutions, how much Santa Fe do we place in God?

❦   ❦   ❦

SECOND MONDAY IN LENT

Abraham, unlike the hero in the Russian fairy tale, knew what to take with him when he and Sarah left their home in obedience to God's call. They took *Santa Fe*, holy faith, as they struck out across the desert toward the fertile crescent and the Armenian mountains. The final destination of Abraham was unknown to him, but he had faith in what God had said to him: "I have given to you a land for you and all your children's children's children." At seventy-five, Abraham didn't even have one child, and his wife was old and barren. To believe in God's promise truly required *Santa Fe*, holy faith.

What better Lenten motto for you and me as we journey through life than "Santa Fe, All the Way." As we wind our way through the confusing labyrinth of life, not sure where we're going or what we're supposed to do here, we need a healthy share of holy faith. The railroad motto could be an ideal mini-prayer for Lent. It can also be the motto for anyone who desires that life be an adventure.

La Santa Fe de la San Francisco, "the Holy Faith of St. Francis." Such a faith is not the kind that deals with dogmas and church doctrines. St. Francis' *Santa Fe* was his deep, abiding trust in God and in God's perpetual providential care. It was the profound conviction that God loved him immensely, that he was one of God's beloved sons. As such he had no doubts that God would take care of him.

That faith of Francis belonged to Abraham, Sarah and a host of other saints. They possessed *Santa Fe*, a holy faith in the Holy and in the Holy's providential care of them. You and I need that same kind of faith to trust in the wisdom of the God who designs the interlacing, intricate patterns of our lives to lead us home.

It would be easy to say, "Well, yes, of course, God spoke directly to Abraham and Sarah, but God doesn't speak to me." Indeed, God does not speak to us from voices out of the clouds. God's usual way is like the language of those who are deaf and blind. God speaks in signs! Blessed are those who can interpret the signs.

God also speaks in braille, in messages that must be felt in the heart. All people of faith have "felt" the message that God has chosen them. However, any who so feel that they are God's beloved are usually judged by the world as insane. They can easily become cult figures and mislead others and themselves. History has proven, however, that St. Francis of Assisi and St. Clare, Saints Abraham and Sarah were not mentally ill. Rather, they were heroes, holy heroes who lived daily lives of adventure. While we have no guarantee as to how history will judge us, we need *Santa Fe* to guide our way along the maze of life.

❁   ❁   ❁

What braille message from God do you feel in your heart this Lenten day? Are you willing and brave enough to follow it?

❁   ❁   ❁

SECOND TUESDAY IN LENT

The very word "adventure" implies risk, fear and danger. Heroes are not people who are not afraid, but those who overcome their fear. While afraid, holy heroes know they live in God, and so they have nothing to fear. Those who choose not to live in God's providence rarely live out adventures; rather, they live venial-ventures. A venial venture is life as a small existence. One lives on a little treadmill: getting up and going to work, coming home and going to bed; getting up and going to work—an endless cycle.

If you don't want your life to be a venial venture, you will have to create the time and the space to go to the mountains. On the mountain top you, like Jesus, can hear the Voice: "You are my beloved." Whenever you take time for prayer, especially time in silence, you climb a mountain, even if you only enter your bedroom or some quiet place. Prayer is the sacred mountain available to all who find time for it.

Whenever we are lost in the labyrinth, instead of climbing a holy mountain of prayer, we usually sit down on some bench. Lost in the maze, we peek around the corner, fearful of what is ahead of us. We sit a lot in life, waiting for some direction. Recently 90% of the population, when asked the question, "What are you living for?" answered, "I'm waiting for something significant to happen!"

People are waiting for various things: their children to grow up and leave home, elderly parents to die, a raise so they can begin to enjoy life.... What are you waiting for—the church to change, good fortune, winning the lottery?

While waiting, you can always excuse yourself from responsibility. "If only I were free of this problem, this burden that weighs me down." It is actually waiting that bogs you down on the path, the waiting that comes from a lack of knowledge about where you are going. If you had an aerial view of the labyrinth, it would be easy to find your way. Most mazes have very high walls which make it impossible to see over them, and so you don't know where you are. Lacking that bird's-eye view of the maze, it is all too easy to feel lost and so to sit down and wait, wait for life to come to you.

If "Santa Fe, All the Way" is a good Lenten mini-prayer, St. Peter gives us another: "Lord, it's good to be here" (Mt. 17: 4). He said those words on the mountain of the transfiguration, but it's a perfect mini-prayer wherever we find ourselves. Whether you're in the midst of some problem or winning a prize, suffering some pain or difficulty, or tasting some delight, to say that being *here* is good is an amazing grace.

It is being present to the whole spectrum of *here* moments, all the blank walls and obstacles as well as the joys and opportunities which arise, that *we* become transfigured! By solving the puzzles of what stands before us, we rise to new levels of being.

❀   ❀   ❀

Take time today to examine some blank walls and dead ends that seem to face you in your life. Are they really dead ends? Should you climb over them, turn around and seek a different route or resign yourself to living with the situation as it is? What did Jesus do when he faced the dead end of the lack of faith in his home village, even among his own family?

❀ ❀ ❀

SECOND WEDNESDAY IN LENT

When faced with the puzzle of a blank wall, one can easily turn it into a wailing wall and moan about bad luck. Instead of wailing, we should pray, "Santa Fe, All the Way" and turn around to try another way. For Peter to say that he found it good to be on top of that mountain was not difficult in the midst of the glory and splendor of a mystical experience. However, Peter couldn't say, "Lord, it's good to be here," when invited to the mountain of Calvary!

He ran away from that mountain. Yet he should have been able to say, "Lord, it is good to be here" when standing at the foot of the cross, just as it was "good to be here" when surrounded by glory.

"Holy Faith, All the Way." "Lord, it's good to be here." It will be your holy faith which tells you that wherever "here" is at this moment in your life is a gift from God since the purpose of each "here" is to transform us. It's customary in Lent to choose penances, acts of self-denial or mortification. Rather than you choosing penances, let life choose them for you. Let God choose the right ones for you, for they are the ones that can best transform you.

A Lenten labyrinth exercise when you wake up in the morning in these forty days is to say, "Lord, it's good to be here." Embrace whatever "here" is for you that day: a difficult marriage, some sickness or pain, a problem, a wonderful little child running around the house or some new task.

The next thing is for *you* to get up and *you* to do something with the gift of the new day. Here we have another Francis as a model. We talked about *Santa Fe de la San Francisco*, the holy faith of St. Francis. Now we can point to a new Francis: Fran Tarkenton. Fran Tarkenton? You mean the famous quarterback of the National Footbal League's Minnesota Vikings? Yes, that's the Francis I mean!

Fran Tarkenton was not only a very successful quarterback, he was also a successful businessman who made over sixty million dollars after leaving football. There's a story from early in his career that's significant for this reflection. When Fran Tarkenton was playing football for the University of Georgia, he was a third-string quarterback sitting on the bench. In the third quarter of a game against Texas in which Georgia was playing terribly, suddenly Fran Tarkenton ran out onto the field. The first string quarterback figured that the coach had sent Fran into the game, so he ran off the field. The coach was horrified because he hadn't ordered a quarterback change. Tarkenton called a play which went for a touchdown. One after another, several more big Tarkenton plays followed and Georgia won the game. The rest, as they say, is history, at least football history.

What impelled Fran Tarkenton off the bench? *Santa*

Fe! He had holy faith in himself that he could win that game, even though he was a third-string quarterback. He had confidence—and he didn't wait for orders. In this Lenten season we're reminded that we are God's chosen ones. We're a prophetic, priestly people. Let's get up off the bench! Let's not wait for something to happen. Let's go and do it.

❀　　❀　　❀

Are you patiently waiting today for "something"? While God's timetable is usually far from ours, what is the point at which we cease waiting and jump up and do what needs to be done? Isn't part of the work of Lent just that—the task of doing what isn't being done because everyone is waiting for orders or for someone else to do it?

❀　　❀　　❀

SECOND THURSDAY IN LENT

It was the third quarter in the life of Jesus when he got up off his bench in Nazareth. He was thirty years old, and since the life expectancy at his time was thirty-five, he was no young man. All about him he saw a conflict raging between light and darkness, good and evil, and it appeared that darkness was winning. Jesus jumped off his village craftsman's bench and plunged into the conflict so that light might become victorious in the world.

You and I spend a lot of our time sitting on the bench, busy at our occupations. Life has not changed much in two thousand years. Darkness, greed and evil ever seem to be winning. Everyone is waiting for orders, waiting for the Pope, the Bishop, the President, the boss, somebody—even God—to tell us what to do. Yet deep down, you and I know what to do. Since each one of us knows what to do, why then don't we do it?

One reason we fail to join actively in the battle against darkness is that we have enough problems within our own workplaces and families. You, like everyone else, have more than enough problems simply making ends meet, keeping bread on the family table and the wolf away from the door, to engage in cosmic battles with evil. If, however, you could strip Jesus of his stained-glass image, pious and other-worldly, you would see a person who also had family problems, who also faced difficulties in making ends meet in his life. As a carpenter or stone mason, like all peasant craftsmen of his day, he was burdened with government taxes—which scholars say consumed almost half the income of the poor. He was further saddled with temple taxes and obligations. As you are tempted to fall back on the various excuses for why you shouldn't get off your bench, realize that Jesus and his early disciples had most of the same excuses and perhaps even more!

Yet Jesus did not call his disciples to go forth on crusades to battle distant evils. Rather he called them to face evil right in their midst. The first place to encounter darkness and evil—and the most dangerous place—is in your heart. Few are willing to explore that dark, mysterious dwelling since to do so could mean not only discovering evil but also might require making radical life changes. It is so much easier to point a finger somewhere else, to look for evil outside yourself: in those with whom you work or live, in your parish, local neighborhood, or society. It is easier to lament and to condemn evil and violence on television, among those who live in the inner-city or in those of other races. After all, nothing is demanded of you personally when you point the finger of accusation outward.

Lent holds the great challenge to reform self, not society. Lent is the season to renew your heart and not the hearts of others. Lent is a time of personal revolution based on the principle that truly evolutionary and revolutionary changes come into the world one by one, heart by heart.

* * *

As you approach the end of this second week of springtime renewal, look at the direction in which your finger of accusation is pointing. Is it pointed at your spouse, friends, co-workers, those in responsible positions or at the world? How often, thus far in Lent, have you found that famous finger pointed at yourself? When it has been, have you found copious good reasons for turning it away?

Experiment today by pointing a finger at yourself and see what reforms such self-examination might be demanding from you.

* * *

SECOND FRIDAY IN LENT

The mere fact that you have entered into this Lenten season as a pilgrim is a sign that you have gotten off your bench! While you might rightly be hesitant about the demands implied in such a holy quest, take encouragement in the very fact that you have begun this sacred journey of renewal and reform. To seek to be a better person, to be more holy, more alive, and to be open to change—the reason for all Lenten labyrinth pilgrimages— is itself a wondrous sign of God's grace.

When Jesus sat on his workshop bench and heard in his heart the call to go down to the Jordan—where John the Baptizer was giving his bath of reform—I wonder if he knew the full implications of that short journey. Perhaps before his Ash Wednesday bath in the Jordan, his intention was to return home to his ordinary life and work. Yet he had the courage to follow the prompting of the Holy Spirit, driving him into the desert so that he could return a radically different person.

Often when we undertake some reform in our lives— whether wanting to lose weight, stop smoking or drinking, or whatever—we have a clear picture of the intended goal of the reform. The mystery of the Lenten labyrinth is that those who enter it are magnetized into a maze which holds the power to change them at the deepest core level. To open yourself to such basic reform—while undertaking some seemingly minor penitential redecoration of your life—is both threatening and a sign of the *amazing* grace of Lent.

Naturally, to begin the process of reforming a place inside that you are unaware even needs to be reformed can create a sense of being lost in the labyrinth. Have faith, however; have *Santa Fe*. As you wander the complicated maze with its twisting pathways, it's easy to feel you are without direction unless you remember your labyrinthian prayer-mantra: "Santa Fe, All the Way."

What is this Holy Faith? It's faith in the truth that you are already home by simply being inside the maze. You have only to reach the center. Remember the words of Saint Catherine of Siena who summed it up so well, "All the way to God is God." God calls you, as God called Moses long ago, to live a holy life. Awakening to where you are when you say "here" makes that call to holiness less difficult than it may seem. And what is that divine design? The puzzling, complicated path of the labyrinth.

❀   ❀   ❀

Do you, like Jesus, sense yourself being pushed by the Holy Spirit along this journey into your Lenten desert of forty days? If you don't, pray for the gift to "feel" that Spirit of the Holy, the consecrator of all works of transformation. If you can feel God's hand upon you, you will also feel the grace to know that any good done during this Lent will be accomplished by God's hand and not yours. Today, simply give yourself over to the amazing grace of the Lenten labyrinth. Simply let go.

Let go into grace not just as a momentary exercise in relaxation. Practice such letting go right in the midst of daily life. The next time you find yourself tempted to moan about the confusion and complexities of life, instead pray one or both of your twin Lenten mini-prayers: "Santa Fe, All the Way," and "Lord, it is good to be here."

❀   ❀   ❀

Second Saturday in Lent

As this second week of Lenten exercises is about to end, a story, a rabbinical parable, provides us with a reflection on the thoughts of this past week.

Once there was a king who constructed a new palace. The palace was actually an enormous maze of complicated passageways and rooms.

In the center of the palace was the throne room where the king sat. When the magnificent palace was completed, the king invited all of his subjects to come and visit him. There was only one doorway into the palace. As the people came in, they were baffled by the sight of countless images of doors and passageways which led outward into further passageways. Whichever way they looked they saw a maze of doorways.

The crowd was confused, and chaos filled the entrance to the palace. Soon everyone turned in frustration and left. When the people were gone, the king's son stepped into the confusing maze-like palace. He also saw nothing but endless passageways leading to more passageways and endless doors leading to even more doors. The prince, however, realized that the entrance to the palace was made of wall-to-wall mirrors reflecting the simplest of designs.

He realized that beyond the mirrors sat his father, the king, who at that moment was directly in front of him. The prince smashed the mirror wall and stepped over the broken glass into the presence of his beloved father.

* * *

Reflect on these three sacred sentences:

> All the way to God is God   (St. Catherine of Siena)
> I am the Way.   (Jesus, in *John's Gospel*)
> From the Unreal lead me to the Real. (The *Upanishads*)

Aware that when you're really on the way you stand face to face with the Divine Mystery, dust off your Santa Fe and look through the confusion of the mirrors of life. See if you can perceive your Beloved sitting calmly on the other side.

> Mirror, mirror on the wall,
> whose face smiles at me after all?

* * *

THIRD SUNDAY IN LENT

As a pilgrim of that very complicated Lenten labyrinth, the Gospel story of Jesus at Jacob's well invites you to rest today. Recall once again the story from John's Gospel. Jesus, passing through Samaria, stops at a well near a Samaritan town which was the site of Jacob's well. Jesus sits down at the well, tired from his journey. At noon a Samaritan woman comes to draw water and Jesus says to her, "Give me a drink."

They were alone because Jesus' disciples had gone off to town to buy some food. The Samaritan woman says, "You are a Jew, and you're asking me, a Samaritan and a woman, for a drink?" Jesus was violating both a social and religious code since Jews had nothing to do with Samaritans.

Jesus then tells her that he is the source of living water. She challenges him that he doesn't even have a bucket and the well is deep. Jesus, in turn, tells her that any who drink the water of that well will be thirsty again, but the water he has to give will cure all thirst. Not only that, they will become fountains of living water themselves!

After she asks for that kind of water, she suspects he is more than just a traveler and asks him about the old Jewish and Samaritan religious debate. "I can see you are a prophet. Our ancestors worshiped on this mountain, but you people claim that Jerusalem is the place where God should be worshiped." Jesus says to her: "Believe me, woman, an hour is coming when you will worship God neither on this mountain nor in Jerusalem. God is spirit, and those who worship God must worship in spirit and in truth." Then Jesus confesses to her that he is the Messiah, and she hurries off to tell the good news to everyone in her village (See Jn. 4: 4-19).

The grace the Samaritan woman was given when she went for water at the well was truly *amazing* grace. The words of that spirited song, *Once I was blind, but now I see*, could have been sung by her. As you travel the Lenten road, you could hum several songs connected with the journey through the maze. "Amazing Grace" speaks of the amazing reality that we've already found our way. Another song that's appropriate for this third Sunday goes, *It's a long way to Tipperary; it's a long way to go.*

It's an Irish ballad written in 1912, but it wasn't successful until 1914 and the outbreak of the First World War. The song is about an Irish lad longing for his home in Tipperary in southern Ireland, heartsick and aware that he would probably never see home again. For British soldiers in the trenches in the First World War it summed up the feelings of weariness and forlornness: *Farewell, Leicester Square. Good-bye, Piccadilly.*

It's a good song for us today, and a song that Jesus could well have sung at Jacob's Well. *It's a long way to Tipperary....* The above Gospel story is what biblical scholars call a "reconstruction." It doesn't appear in the other three Gospels, yet it's very important because it has wonderful insights for any of us who feel weary and tired. It's a *long* way to Tipperary, whether Tipperary is another name for holiness or enlightenment, or being free of childhood scars.

❀   ❀   ❀

This Sunday helps you reflect on what makes you weary in life. Are you weary of seemingly unresolvable conflicts both personally and globally? Do you feel forlorn about your progress in the spiritual life? Lent is only two weeks old; are you perhaps already growing weary of it? If Jesus rested when he felt weary and tired, isn't that permission for you to do the same? Without guilt and as a Lenten exercise, rest from work today.

"Let us strive, then, to enter into God's rest" (Heb. 4:11).

❀   ❀   ❀

THIRD MONDAY IN LENT

After yesterday's rest—as Jesus rested at Jacob's well—it's time to take up your cross and begin again your journey in the Lenten labyrinth. Today's reflection is a parable that speaks to that journey.

Once upon a time there was a little railroad steam locomotive named Santa Fe Annie who labored long and hard across the prairies, pulling endless trains of boxcars on the *Atchison, Topeka and Santa Fe*. Huffing and puffing, she also pulled long trains of passenger cars up and down the mountain—doing her duty as all railroad locomotives are supposed to do.

One day Annie had a Zen-like moment of enlightenment. She said, "I'm being railroaded! I don't have any other options of where I can go. I *have* to follow the tracks." First Annie was angry, then sad, then depressed.

In the Kansas City railroad yard she shared her new awareness with a few of her friends, locomotives from the Union Pacific, the Great Northwestern, the New York Central and Southern Pacific railroads. When she told them, they gasped in shock. A couple even blew their whistles. "Wheewow, girl! What are you talking about? Who do you think you are? We don't make the rules about where the tracks go. Just follow them! That's life!"

Santa Fe Annie resigned herself to her fate, yet she still wished with all her heart to be derailed. When she listened to her heart, Annie was fearful: could she make it in life? I mean, without following the tracks.

One day, tired and thirsty, she huffed and puffed into a little jerkwater town in Kansas. She wished out loud, "Oh, some day that I might be free not to have to follow these boring tracks." As she jerked down the spout on the water tank (that's how those jerkwater towns got their name), to her surprise a voice came from high above:

"Santa Fe Annie, your wish can come true, if you but remember!"

She looked up with wonder at the skies—actually at the water tank from which came the voice—and said, "Remember?"

"Yes," said the mysterious voice. "Remember what's printed on you and on your boxcars—and up here on me, this railroad water tank."

Annie looked up and read aloud, "Santa Fe, All the Way."

"Yes," said the voice, "the city's name is short for the original Spanish, *Villa Real de la Santa Fe de la San Francisco*, 'the Royal City of the Holy Faith of St. Francis.' Annie, the slogan of your railroad is the secret to your wish. Have holy faith that God does not want you to be railroaded in life. Santa Fe, All the Way, Annie. Just do it!"

Filled with water, Santa Fe Annie put on a full head of steam and jumped the tracks. Yes, she jumped those boring tracks she'd followed for years and huffed and puffed her way down some delightful country roads. "What fun! What excitement! What joy!" she said to herself—until a farmer saw her coming down his road with fire and black smoke pouring out of her stacks, great clouds of silvery steam billowing out from beneath her.

The farmer screamed with terror and ran into town shouting, "A great monster, a fire-breathing monster's comin' down the old Meagher Road." Quickly, a crowd gathered at the edge of town, armed with shotguns and rifles. When Santa Fe Annie came huffing and puffing into sight, they opened fire. As bullets zinged and zanged through her iron skin, she screeched to a stop. Throwing herself into full reverse at top speed, she backed up all the way to the forest.

Hiding in the deep forest, she rested and nursed her wounds, the numerous gaping bullet holes in her skin. As she did, she had a second Zen-like enlightenment. "Stop, look, listen. Be prudent where, when and with whom you enjoy the fun of being derailed."

❀ ❀ ❀

Your labyrinth exercise today is to ask yourself if the parable of Santa Fe Annie has any personal implications.

❀ ❀ ❀

THIRD TUESDAY IN LENT

It's easy, on our way to God, to feel that there are few if any options but to follow those iron rails laid down by religion and society. While well traveled, they can be so boring! No wonder kids don't want to go to church. They know the truth: it *is* boring.

Good news, though, at the banner headline: *Jesus Was Tired*! It's truly good news that Jesus felt like a flat tire, which is something you and I also have felt. It's such good news because he stopped and rested! Instead of Jesus' usual stance of being the servant to others, at the Samaritan well the disciples went to get bread for him. It's hard for us in this culture to rest, even on the day of rest, Sunday. We're all so busy. It seems that all of life's traffic lights are stuck on green.

There never seem to be any red lights that allow us to stop, except when we're sick and forced to bed for rest. We're on the go perpetually. In this Lenten season— when, once upon a time, it was scratchy hairshirts, black fasts, meatless meals, long evening services in church— maybe there is a new, painful Lenten penance, worse than needles under your fingernails. The new penance is to *stop*. That's right, do nothing, just stop.

Pope John Paul II in a Lenten talk said, "We are asked to remove ourselves, in so far as possible, from the often frantic rhythm of modern existence, to review our whole life in the light of the Word of God." "In so far as it is possible...." Indeed, we live frantic existences. But it's not wrong to rest in the labyrinth, to find a bench or chair and rest. We need to stop in order to see if we're being railroaded in life, trapped on tracks that lead nowhere.

❋   ❋   ❋

Let your Lenten reflection today be to ask yourself if you feel like you're being railroaded in life. Like Santa Fe Annie, do you feel trapped on tracks that lead nowhere?

Those who never stop, who never rest, cannot lead reflective lives and so are unable to make necessary changes in lifestyle and behavior. Take time, stop and reflect.

❋   ❋   ❋

THIRD WEDNESDAY IN LENT

The writer of *Hebrews* said that disciples should learn how to rest, should have the faith to rest:

> Today, if you should hear God's voice, harden not your hearts as at the revolt when your ancestors tested and tried me. Because I was angered with that generation and I said, "They have always been of erring heart"; I swore in my anger, "They shall never enter my rest." It was their faithlessness that kept them from entering. We have indeed heard the good news, as they did. But the word which they heard did not profit them, for they did not receive it in faith. It is we who have believed who enter into that rest (Heb. 3: 7-8, 9-11, 19; 4: 2-3).

In your Lenten journey you need to have faith that the labyrinth, the complicated maze you're traveling, is just like an interstate highway and also has rest areas. There are times to pull off the path and stop to rest. Also, just as contemporary rest areas on interstate highways usually have water fountains, the mystical maze has its wells—which may be wishing wells!

Where do you find these resting places? Well, an empty chapel or your prayer corner (a corner of your bedroom or den set aside for prayer) is a "Rest Room." All churches are or should be Rest Rooms, if they can be kept quiet and restful, instead of perpetually filled with activity. They can be places of holy rest if you can come to them early and leave late.

Furthermore, every home should have its own Rest Room. Recent studies show that 85% of Americans are "clocklocked." It's a new term, like gridlocked and deadlocked. Clocklocked: 85% of Americans have no spare time, no time to make love, no time to pray. No wonder all of us are so weary.

❀　　❀　　❀

If among your Lenten resolutions there was not one about slowing down, begin now to take more time for yourself. Find more time to pray, time to spend with family or friends. It's not too late, even on this third Wednesday in Lent, to make such a reform resolution.

Remember: you begin each day with all the time in the world. If you lack time for the truly essential things in life, then perhaps you need to set new priorities. You can choose how you spend your time. Take time now to examine how to budget your bank account of time.

❀　　❀　　❀

THIRD THURSDAY IN LENT

I have a feeling that there was something more than just being tired that made Jesus stop at the Samaritan well. Wells were both social and sacred places. They were social places because people came to visit and share gossip there.

They were sacred, like the well in the Gospel story, not only because many were dug by spiritual leaders, but because whatever is scarce in life is sacred.

Money is scarce, and that's why banks tend to look a good deal like churches. They're very "holy" places; you even whisper in banks. Ever since the days of John Calvin, we've treated banks as such sacred spots since wealth has become accepted as a sign of God's blessing on those who work hard and keep the commandments. In Jesus' homeland, water was scarce—and as valuable as gold.

Once it was believed that all pools and wells had a guardian spirit, a goddess or nymph. When you went to the well, you gave a gift and then made a wish to the guardian spirit. Today, even at wishing wells in shopping malls, the custom is to throw money into them for some charity or simply for good luck. We perform this ritual without knowing that we're involved in the very sacred, ancient ritual of gifting the goddess of the well.

❧   ❧   ❧

If you were to come upon one of those magical wishing wells, what would you ask the guardian nymph to grant you? If you can't think of anything specific, consider throwing a significant gift of money or time into some worthwhile project!

As with those ancient wishing wells, you might be surprised at what gift you would be given in return! This reflection on wishing wells can be a reminder to perform the classic Lenten work of giving alms and performing acts of charity.

❧   ❧   ❧

THIRD FRIDAY IN LENT

The well of Jacob at which Jesus stopped—I propose to you—was a wishing well. It was a well where an unusual experience happened. Even though the story at the well is a reconstruction, it is perfectly in tune with the culture. The lives of men and women in Jesus' day were very sharply divided. Women only came to the well in the morning and at sunset. The rest of the time was set aside for men to visit there.

The woman came at noon—the brazen hussy! It was also, probably, because she was being shunned by the other women. She was shunned because she had been married five times and was living with somebody else at the moment. Yet, even though she was a shameful woman in the eyes of her community, Jesus did not treat her like a brazen hussy in their encounter. Quite the contrary! The scripture scholar Dr. John Pilch says that she is the most thoroughly catechized person in all of Scripture! Jesus, like a good teacher, leads her slowly, one step at a time, from darkness to enlightenment.

Now the question is, why did he ask her for a drink—something forbidden to a Jew? Why did he as a Jew and a member of his society even engage in a conversation with her? A *woman*—and not even Jewish! How was Jesus, like Santa Fe Annie in Monday's parable, able to be derailed from the strict lines of the religious and cultural tracks he was supposed to be riding on?

As you ponder the out-of-character behavior of Jesus, at least out of character for a Jewish man of his time, remember that he was tired. I propose to you that, at the well, Jesus was not so much meek and humble of heart as sick and tired of heart. He was sick and tired, fed up with the silly laws that separate people, laws that brand women as inferior. He was sick and tired of those religious debates about which religion is superior to all others, the "Mine is the best" attitude.

Was Jesus also sick and tired of the fact that any group of people thought they could capture God and put God inside some little building on this or that mountain? His words to the woman at Jacob's well seemed edged in impatience. Jesus said that God is Spirit, and so you cannot put God in any box or house. You cannot put God on a leash like a pet and say, "This is my God. Don't you pet my God."

How was Jacob's well a wishing well? The truths that Jesus shared with the woman were truly unique, yet she understood all that he said. How his heart must have danced with delight when, without being told, she raced off to the village square to tell her people the good news.

The brazen hussy—to go and tell the men what she had experienced! Only men gathered in the village square. Like Santa Fe Annie, she jumped the tracks that society had laid down. The Samaritan woman had *Santa Fe*, faith in God and in herself. That faith set her on fire with the message. The delight of the story at Jacob's wishing well is that her wishes and those of Jesus came true.

Jesus, being both hungry and thirsty, provides anyone who enters the maze with two general rules. If you recall, the English have a great fondness for mazes. In England there are over a hundred mazes with high hedges. You can easily get lost in them for hours. The first rule for entering one is: "Never go in a maze that does not have beer stalls and sandwich stands to nourish lost and weary travelers!" The second rule for a mystic maze is: "They all have wishing wells, for those with eyes of *Santa Fe*."

If you wish to find the well in this Lenten labyrinth, sit down and rest. In the silence of sitting, the divine well of God's love will both nourish and refresh you.

❀   ❀   ❀

Friday is a day to abstain from meat and perhaps to fast. This Lenten Friday, however, may be just the day not to abstain. One of the reasons for fasting and abstaining in Lent is to curb voracious appetites so we can again appreciate the giftedness of even the most simple things in life. Yet Lent is also a time to stop and create space to be truly nourished. What nourishes you on the journey of life? The paradox is that fine music, fine art and fine food can nourish us deeply.

Sometimes guilt creeps into our soul when we feel that this or that luxury, while nourishing, is not proper. Yet, only those who are rich inwardly are able to be truly simple.

While Lent is a time traditionally to give up something we enjoy, it can also be the time to take up—with purity—that which we enjoy most and which nourishes us most deeply.

❀   ❀   ❀

THIRD SATURDAY IN LENT

Into the silence of this Jewish Day of Rest and Worship, we drop the bucket of our hearts and let it go down and down and down. We don't worry if we can't meditate: "Oh, I can't keep my mind still." As long as we're sitting still, we're being nourished on some level. Whenever we feel that *It's a long way to Tipperary*—and that we'll never make it—it's time to rejoice. We rejoice because we know that God does not carry a stopwatch. God is not timing us. It's not like measuring up in some marathon. No, God does not use a stopwatch.

So when you sit down and do nothing, and you see one of those zealous spiritual seekers racing by, panting on his or her way to this workshop or that form of enlightenment, don't worry. God's not timing us. When you see those battalions of Fundamentalist Christians clutching their bibles, singing, "Onward, Christian soldiers...," don't feel guilty sitting there, doing nothing. Have holy faith that you're already there! Once you're inside of the maze, the whole maze is divine. Remember the words of St. Catherine of Siena, "All the way to God *is* God," and the words of Jesus, "I am the Way."

Pilgrims on their way to Mecca go very much in the pattern of the very complicated circular design of the labyrinth. In Mecca, in the middle of a great square, is the Kaaba, a giant black stone. The belief in Islam is that the angel Gabriel gave it to Abraham. Islamic pilgrims march around and around it in prayerful procession. A Muslim mystic said, "I used to go around and around and around the Kaaba until I attained God, and then I realized God was going around and around and around me." To this St. Gregory of Nyssa added, "To seek perfection *is* perfection."

So regardless of what kind of watch you have, make it a different kind of stopwatch. Stop frequently in life and do nothing, mindful that when you can stop your watch God will nourish you.

This Lenten Saturday reflection concludes with a rabbinical parable:

> The disciples of a rabbi came to him, and they asked about the *zaddik*, zealous people who work themselves into a frenzy to reach ecstasy and religious enlightenment. So he told them this story.
>
> Once a king created a great maze of complicated passageways. He then sat in the center of the maze and told his followers to come to him. Those who came were of two types. The first group entered the maze with sledgehammers and crowbars. They forced their way to the center. The second group came in very quietly and gently, wandering around the maze. Whenever they came to a complicated, twisted turn, they wrote out a little message and left it there for those who were to come after them.
>
> The rabbi said that those of the first group were obsessed with the command of the king to come to him. Those of the second group, conversely, had faith in the great mercy of the king. They had faith that the king would magnetically draw them to himself.

❀   ❀   ❀

This rabbinical story provides a wonderful Lenten exercise. You could call the little notes the second group left behind "labyrinthian Lenten messages." Such notes could be left on the bus, under a pillow, on an office desk or stuck in a bottle and tossed in a river. They would be little messages of hope and encouragement for others who, like us, are wandering the maze.

Create your own labyrinthian Lenten messages. Here are a few examples that could be written on small pieces of paper:

Criticism is not punishment, praise is not reward. They're simply information necessary to improve performance.

or

Every second of your life is precious. Stop your watch and enjoy life.

or

While your watch is set for this time zone, live as if it were the year 2050, as if the future were already here.

❀   ❀   ❀

FOURTH SUNDAY IN LENT

For this stage of your Lenten journey, remember to take along your walking staff, for you are moving to the next level of the labyrinth. A walking stick is a good symbol of your discipleship. When Jesus sent his disciples to proclaim the gospel, he told them, "Take nothing with you, no billfold, no money, no food, only your walking staffs" (Mk. 6: 8).

Today you will move more deeply into what the poet Milton called "the blind mazes of the tangled wood." As you do, you're given a unique walking stick. It's not the kind of staff the disciples used but another familiar walking stick: a white stick with the red tip, the sign that the walker is blind.

The complicated maze is difficult enough; imagine attempting to travel it by listening carefully as you tap-tap-tap your way through the maze. The labyrinth is filled with cul-de-sacs, blind alleys in which there is no eye, no passageway out. A good patron saint to pray to as you tap-tap-tap your way with your white cane is the blind beggar

Jesus cured in John's Gospel story (Jn. 9).

He had a blind date with destiny when Jesus healed him since he didn't even know who it was who gave him the gift of sight. The gift of sight is a perfect one to pray for in this Lenten season. The Letter to the Ephesians says, "There was a time when you were in darkness, but now you are in the light in God. Well, then, live as children of light" (Eph. 5: 8).

The blind beggar was a child of darkness, blind from birth. He was made a child of light by Jesus in more ways than sight. Prophecy had foretold that giving sight to the blind was to be a wonder-work of the Messiah when he came. Luke's Gospel, filled with cures of blind people, suggests that the blindness to be cured by the Messiah comes in many forms.

❧ ❧ ❧

On this first day of a new week in your Lenten pilgrimage, ask yourself in what ways you might be blind. Are there aspects of yourself, certain behavior characteristics, about which you are unsighted? Do you blind yourself to injustices in your community or in your church? Are you God-blind? Are you able to see God's glory, which Isaiah said filled all of heaven and earth?

Take time, perhaps with your eyes closed, to quietly explore the various ways in which you are unseeing.

❧ ❧ ❧

FOURTH MONDAY IN LENT

This week's Lenten reflection deals with the blind beggar whom Jesus cured. So ask yourself, "Am I as blind as a bat?" Before you answer, remember that bats aren't really blind! Those nocturnal mammals can, however, suggest a type of blindness from which you can be cured—if you truly wish to see.

That lack of sight is not blindness from birth, congenital blindness, but *congenial* blindness. Related to the word *genial* which means kindly and friendly, congenial means suited to one's taste.

In John's account of the healing, the beggar was congenitally blind, but the Pharisees had congenial blindness. They were blinded by their religion. They could not comprehend how a work of divine healing could occur on the Sabbath! That was a day when any kind of work was forbidden since it was a day of holy rest.

The Pharisees can be symbolic of anyone who is blinded by religion. However, they were not the only ones afflicted in the Gospel story. The blind man's parents were also congenially blind. They rejected any responsibility because they didn't want to be thrown out of their worship place.

How often have you been congenially blind—even in small things? For example, if an electric light is left on in a room, do you say, "I didn't turn the light on. It's not my responsibility to turn it off!" If you see trash on the floor or on the side of the highway, do you say to yourself, "I didn't put it there! Let the janitor or the street workers pick it up." A brief but honest examination of conscience could reveal many occasions when you've turned a blind eye to life.

❀　　❀　　❀

Take a few minutes now to look back over the past few days and see if you can recall occasions or events when you were congenially, conveniently, blind or deaf? Perhaps you saw someone being shamed and pretended not to see, not wanting to be involved. Have you walked past someone begging and not only turned a blind eye but turned your heart to stone, giving not even a silent blessing to the person in need? As a work of Lenten reform, examine carefully any occasions when you may have suffered from congenial blindness.

❀　　❀　　❀

FOURTH TUESDAY IN LENT

If given an option, would you choose to go through life as if you were attending a Blindman's Banquet? That expression comes from a medieval story about twelve blind beggars who came to a castle begging for alms.

The lord of the castle came out and addressed the blind beggars who had come to his gates, "Well, well, my good men, I understand you are in need. Go now to the village. Eat, drink and be merry. Here are twenty gold coins for you." The beggars all tapped their canes in delight, saying, "Oh, thank you, thank you. God bless you, Sir," and they went directly to the inn. There they enjoyed a wonderful feast of good food and drink.

After they had all they desired, the inn keeper presented the bill for their banquet. Each of the blind men said, pointing to the beggar in the next seat, "Give it to him, he's got the money." As it happened, none of the beggars had been given any gold! Each one thought someone else had received the bag of gold coins from the lord of the castle, and so the inn keeper's bill was just passed from one to another.

Are you and I tempted to attend such a feast with no responsibility for its cost? We want good highways, good police protection, excellent schools and weekly garbage pick-up—but without having to pay for them. Like the beggars in the story, we say, "Let *them* pay for it": "them" meaning the state, the rich or anyone but ourselves paying. Church and state equally suffer from parasites, who like blind beggars ask for good service yet are blind to their share of the cost.

We can be like blind beggars in the labyrinth. Being blind, it's easy to bump into another, easy to accidentally break things—like another's heart. But you may object, "I'm not blind. I'm a child of light, I see because I've been redeemed by Jesus. I am not blind!" If you find that you are disturbed by being called blind, then look in the mirror!

Look closely to see if you are wearing the kind of dark glasses that make you color blind. What do you see when you look at others who are black-skinned or yellow-skinned? Does your behavior change when you see that you are dealing with foreigners or aliens? If so, then perhaps you do have a vision affliction.

Look again into your Lenten mirror and ask yourself, "Do I wear dark glasses with a large cross on each lens, or a star of David?" Just as you can wear dark glasses that separate you from people of other races or nationalities, so you can wear dark glasses that make you religiously or spiritually vision impaired. Being spiritually blind is a form of defective sight that makes other people's religions appear to you as inherently false, inferior and even diabolical.

You can also see with a vision that distorts those of a gender or sexual orientation other than yours. What do you see when you look at young people, at those of advanced age? If you view them with a distorted vision, it's only logical that you will treat them differently.

❁   ❁   ❁

Ask yourself again the questions found in this Lenten reflection. Take your time to look at each one of them, even if doing so makes you feel uncomfortable. Such questions can be like hair shirts as they painfully prick your conscience. But, like old-fashioned Lenten hair shirts, they can be the kind of good penance that leads to true reform and renewal of your life.

❁   ❁   ❁

FOURTH WEDNESDAY IN LENT

If by the middle of this week you've accepted the fact that you *might* suffer from congenial and convenient blindness, your next step would be to seek some cure for it. A good spring cure could be like the one that Jesus used on the blind beggar, a little homeopathic folk medicine.

Jesus took some dirt, spat on it and made a mud paste which he spread on the blind man's eyes. To smear mud on another's eyes might seem like strange medicine, unless you know that in the ancient world the saliva of a holy man was considered to be extremely magical and curative! Saliva was looked upon as a kind of sacrament of cleansing. The second part of the cure was also an act of cleansing: the blind man was told to go to the pool and wash.

You can be cured of your blindness by considering another old medical treatment dealing with cleansing. During the sixteenth to the mid-nineteenth centuries there was a craze much like today's health food and dieting fads. It was thought to be the great cure-all for all forms of sickness, from bad complexion to depression. To receive this miracle medical healing you simply called for two pharmacists: "*Limonadiers des posterieurs!*" which is French for "Call for the lemonaders of the rear end!"

In the court of Louis XIV, in which French culture reached its zenith of refinement and artistic splendor, the king, nobility and all of the wealthy were daily visited by the lemonaders. Two or more pharmacists arrived and administered enemas. It was not uncommon to have more than one a day! King Louis XIII who was ill much of his life had two a day, except on holidays and holy days, and King Louis XIV had four enemas daily.

Among the ingredients used for the enemas were rosemary, thyme and orange blossom. Not only were these herbal enemas considered curative for just about everything, but the more enemas the better! In the middle-age of life when the sexual energies quieted down, one could have a *restaurant*. That French word means "restorative" and originally referred to a nicotine enema.

Would you care for a Lenten enema? Perhaps such a new medical cure might be featured soon in *The New England Journal of Medicine* as a cure for congenial blindness. To be cured of congenial blindness, color and ethnic blindness, even church blindness or any of the various other types of distortion of sight, maybe just the thing is an enema!

If you are a Roman Catholic, know that the Pope wants you to have an enema! Pope John Paul II, in a Lenten sermon about the spiritual journey, said, "Only through an authentic journey of inner purification will it be possible to have a full experience of Easter and rise with the Lord to new life." An inner purification is at the core of the cure for blindness, especially if you wish to experience a "full Easter"!

If you are a Protestant, you may say, "Thank God I'm not a Catholic!" If you are a Catholic, you may say, "Well, I'm not into papal requests." However you might object, consider also the ancient wisdom from the *Tao Te Ching* of China, written about two and one-half thousand years ago. In Chapter twenty-two the text says, "Yield and overcome; bend and be straightened; *empty* and be full."

Empty yourself of all the stuff that blinds you, such

as old prejudices and subtle forms of discrimination based on money, education or religious attitudes. Empty yourself of as many of these elements as possible so you can know a full Easter and a full life.

Such emptiness is important. John Paul II in that Lenten sermon said, "Contemporary men and women seem particularly sensitive to the need for transparency and authenticity in life." You may nod in agreement, but do you really want to be so transparent as to have all that's inside of you made visible? In a way, you and I are transparent whether we want to be or not. For those "with eyes to see," our behavior and our speech reveal what's inside of us.

❀   ❀   ❀

Enemas—whether physical or spiritual—are not fun! Only when what's inside of us makes us sick, would we submit to an enema. Pray for God-sight so you may see clearly the sicknesses within you and in the world that bring suffering.

Pray on this Lenten day that all illnesses caused by the blindness of discrimination based on religion, race, gender, sexual orientation, social class or education may be flushed out of your heart. Pray for the Lenten grace to be cleansed each time you find that you're blinded by some negative thought or memory.

❀   ❀   ❀

FOURTH THURSDAY IN LENT

An old expression implies that love wears dark glasses and carries a white cane. "Love is blind," but blinder than love is hate, especially when it takes the form of color blindness or church blindness. Besides various cultural or religious discriminations, *memories* can also blind us.

The dark glasses of persons blinded by memories have mirrored lenses through which they always look backwards. Memory blindness is quite popular today as a way to avoid personal responsibility. "Oh, I was abused as a child!" Or, "My family was dysfunctional." Indeed, there are many valid cases of child abuse, but there is also an abundance today of what professionals call false memories.

Those who are unhappy, who lament because they aren't living the kind of lives they want to live, can create or augment memories of being abused or neglected as children. These memories are like coloring books: usually they are just outlines. Yet they can be colored in to make others responsible for present unhappiness. It's a convenient coping mechanism to remove responsibility for patterns of personal behavior or for one's present state of unhappiness.

There's a well-known adage, "The victors in life write history." That's true. Read any history book and you'll see that whoever won the war wrote the history of the war. Today, however, the losers in life are busy writing their own histories as they reconstruct their childhoods or their marriages in a way that justifies their present state of unhappiness or pain. The coloration of the memories is in proportion to the size of the problem or the inability to deal with it.

Paul's Letter to the Ephesians tells us:

> There was a time when you were in darkness, but now you are the light in God. Well, then, live as children of light. Light produces every kind of goodness and justice and truth. Be correct in your judgment of what pleases God. Take no part in vain deeds done in darkness; rather, condemn them. It is shameful even to mention the things these people do in secret (Eph. 5: 8-12).

Those shameful things done in secret are not necessarily acts performed in some darkened bedroom. More likely they are the shameful thoughts with which we play in the back rooms of our minds. Such thoughts breed deeds of darkness. The writer of *Ephesians*, continues:

> But when such deeds are condemned, they are seen in the light of day, and all that then appears is light. That is why we read: "Awake, O sleeper, arise from the dead, and Christ will give you light" (Eph. 5: 13-14).

❧　❧　❧

Lent is a spiritual season of purification which encourages you to undertake a good spring housecleaning—of your mind. However, a single act of whitewashing thoughts that are dark and dangerous won't do it. Our thoughts are like mice, creatures of habit and routine. After they are driven out, they quickly return to their nesting places in your home. A complete change of mind patterns requires daily purification. Be on your guard with your thoughts. While hidden from view, they readily find expression in words and deeds.

Nourish today the desire to have only the kind of thoughts you believe God would find pleasing, since such good thoughts are healthy for you, others and the world.

❀   ❀   ❀

FOURTH FRIDAY IN LENT

From the sixteenth to the mid-nineteenth centuries enemas were thought to be the cure-all because the common opinion was that human waste inside of you poisons you. The idea was to get it out as soon as possible! They got it out four times a day—if they could afford it. Today, you might smile at this notion or the belief that mud and the saliva of a holy man might cure blindness. Yet would you doubt that hate, anger, bearing a grudge, being resentful or dwelling on false memories, and even valid memories, can blind you?

Another form of blindness involves shadowy vision. Instead of seeing what is really there, one produces negative images—usually from one's own soul—and then projects them onto others. Negative projections are focused onto Jews and Gentiles, African Americans and Mexican Americans, women and men, believers and non-believers. Such projections cause one's vision to be distorted. If you suffer from projection-vision—or are the victim of it—you may ask, "Doesn't some cure exist for those projected images that distort vision?"

Yes, there is a cure for this and other forms of spiritual blindness. The cure is to have a Lenten enema! This variety of enema is made not with orange blossoms, nicotine or even holy water. It's an out-of-style recipe: go to confession! It's out-of-style, that is, unless you pay fifty dollars an hour to go to confession; then it's "in." However, the kind of purification contained in the confession of faults doesn't have full effect when confessing only to some third party. The essence of healing occurs when you go to confession to the person(s) you have injured.

Whatever it is that you need to confess, get it out of you. It's not just a matter of health. Know that you will never reach the center of the labyrinth without this kind of enema. True sorrow empties guilt, and wholehearted forgiveness empties out anger. While you may say, "I have already forgiven my parents and my ex-wife (or whoever)" if you find yourself reacting to persons or situations based on old childhood memories, you are still disabled because those memories haven't been purged of their destructive elements. Be patient with yourself, however, for it takes time and daily discipline.

The old opinion was that human waste within a person is poisonous. In that old folk medical view is a grain of truth. Indeed, what fills us tends to both poison and define us! What a typical enema removes provides a good image for what we become when we allow dangerous and negative thoughts to nest in our hearts and heads. Regardless of how beautiful or carefully applied is our makeup, we are what fills us!

As a child of light, live in the light. Living in the light involves living today. Regardless of your childhood, regardless of what kind of marriage you once had, they are in the past. Live today. Be responsible for your behavior today and live in the light. Yet take heart if you find it difficult to "live in the light." If it seems impossible to live in light, then call for the lemonade man and get out of you whatever is causing you to live in darkness.

Cleanse yourself of any hatred and resentment toward your parents, former or present spouses, or the church. Be on your guard and refuse to enjoy the feeling of nesting anger inside of you, hugging your sense of being a victim to negatively empower yourself. With love for those who injured you, with love for yourself, with love for God, get rid of it, whatever *it* happens to be!

❀　　❀　　❀

With great gentleness, search carefully the back rooms of your mind for any ugly and deformed memories that may be poisoning you today. If you always find something wrong with those who are in positions of authority in your life, look carefully for some lost memory of a parent or teacher with whom you are still not reconciled. Seek healing even with those who are dead.

With great love and patience, follow carefully the long and often crooked roots of today's impatience and anger until you find the source of your brooding rage. Then have yourself a good Lenten enema.

❀　　❀　　❀

FOURTH SATURDAY IN LENT

Saint Peter, concerned about good health, asked Jesus, "Lord, how many enemas shall I have, seven?" "No, Peter," Jesus replied, "not seven enemas, seventy times seven enemas—if necessary" (See Mt. 18: 21-22). Jesus later added a piece of very good practical medical advice when he was talking about an evil spirit which had been driven out of a person.

He said that the expelled dark spirit wandered out in the desert, looking for a place to nest. Not finding any, the evil spirit came back and found that the house from which it had been purged had been swept clean by a good enema. So it went out and got seven spirits who were more evil that it was, and moved back into the house. Jesus said that the last state of the person who had been cleansed was now worse than before getting the enema (See Lk. 11: 24-26).

It is not sufficient to remove bad memories, be they false or valid. It's not enough to remove the darkness of the desire for what is harmful. Once you've had a good enema and cleansed yourself of evil, you must fill yourself with light, which is to say justice, peace and love. They are the residents of your heart that insure there will be no room for hate or anger.

As today concludes another Lenten week, recall this week's theme of blindness and the cure required if you are to be a child of light. Remember the wisdom of the *Tao Te Ching* of ancient China, "Empty yourself so as to be full." Add to those words, the message of Pope John Paul II, "The journey of life is one of interior purification." And to these two add the famous words about non-violence and peace: "Turn the other cheek"!

"Turn the other cheek" as Louis XIII and Louis XIV did two to four times a day, seek to be purified as often as necessary. As you do, keep before you what might be the most unique of all beatitudes: "Blessed are those who have frequent enemas, for they shall enjoy the Kingdom of God here and in the hereafter—and they will not have to use white canes."

❀   ❀   ❀

Ponder the words of Jesus to the Pharisees, who were offended at his implication that they were blind: "If you were blind, there would be no sin in that. But you say, 'We see,' and so your sin remains" (Jn. 9: 41).

While some truth about yourself may be apparent to others, you can easily be blind to it. What realities do you refuse to acknowledge as true? In those realities, are you guilty of rejecting the design and will of God?

❀   ❀   ❀

FIFTH SUNDAY IN LENT

Entering into this fifth week of Lent, you are faced with two questions as the path before you suddenly descends below the surface into the underground. The path is littered with bones and the oppressive stench of death, as the first question taps you on the shoulder, "Where's the closest exit?" Inner purification, renewal of spiritual disciplines and working at living a better life are all activities that are wholesome. On the other hand, the smell of death on this fifth week makes one want to drop out of this labyrinth as soon as possible.

Since the path of the maze is descending, it signals the movement into another level of Lent. That change of direction leads to a second question, which appears almost every morning: "What shall I wear today?"

What should a devout pilgrim of the last two weeks of Lent wear? What is appropriate attire for wandering in an underground maze that is also a tomb? The original labyrinths were royal tombs in Egypt, partly above ground and partly below. The purpose of the complicated maze was to present a confusing path to those who entered, making it nearly impossible to find the tombs of the Pharaohs and nobility. These burial mazes offer quite a contrast to the delightful green hedgerow mazes found in England, which are open to the sun and the blue sky.

The labyrinths of ancient Egypt were very frightening places. Once a person entered one, he or she rarely came out alive. This bit of history provides some background for the Greek mythical story of the hero Theseus. The King of Crete, Minos, created a magnificent labyrinth, in the center of which he placed a flesh-eating monster, the Minotaur. The beast had the head of a bull and the body of a man—and a great hunger to feast on human flesh. Each year the King of Crete demanded from Greece a tribute of seven handsome young men and seven beautiful young women whom he sent into the maze. None of them were ever able to elude the beast that lurked in the labyrinth and come out of the maze alive.

Before being sent into the maze, the Greek hero Theseus was befriended by the daughter of Crete's king. She gave him a large ball of thread and told him to unravel the cord as he entered the maze so that once he got to the center he could find his way back out. Theseus killed the Minotaur and followed the cord back safely out of the labyrinth. This story from Greek mythology is an overture to Easter. Jesus, the new Theseus, entered the labyrinth of death, killed the beast and escaped alive.

❀   ❀   ❀

As you enter today into this final stage of Lent, reflect on how you and everyone born into this life journeys through that labyrinth of death. You and I long for the kind of gift given to

Theseus, a ball of string that will enable us to find our way out alive.

Perhaps you already have such a ball of string! Jesus reminded Martha that she had one. He implied that her brother Lazarus had been buried with one when he said to her,

> I am the Resurrection and the life:
> whoever believes in me,
>> even though they should die,
>> will come to life;
> and whoever is alive and believes in me
>> will never die.
> Do you believe this?
> "Yes, Lord," she replied.

(Jn. 11: 25-27)

Can you hold onto those words with faith like a life-giving string and allow them, and your love for God, to lead you out of the fear of death? If Jesus' words fail to give you a sense of security, this fifth Sunday in Lent would be a good time to explore your fears and doubts about death and resurrection.

❀   ❀   ❀

FIFTH MONDAY IN LENT

Life is indeed a complex and puzzling labyrinth. When you're young, it's fun and challenging to play with that puzzle. When you're young, life is about today; it's about vitality and is filled with promise. At a certain point in life, however, you make a turn in the maze. You realize, then, where the path is leading you. The maze of life, even from the moment of birth, is a funeral labyrinth which leads in only one direction—to the center pit where lives the flesh-eating beast.

At whatever age you wake up and make that terrible discovery, in panic, you plead, "Where's the nearest exit?" You realize, however, without anyone telling you, that there is only one exit: death! Once you enter the labyrinth there is no way out, nor is there a way to go back from where you came. There is no fountain of youth. While the human mind is ingenious in its ability to deny the truth, the further you travel this path the faster you are drawn to the center—and your death. Daily you fall faster and faster toward the center, drawn by death's gravity.

"From the unreal, lead me to the real," is the beautiful Hindu prayer which confronts this great denial. This prayer is a perfect companion at this fearful stage of the labyrinth. To live life fully, you must confront the reality of a death, which, regardless of your age, always comes too soon! When teenagers die, there is the great lament: "Oh, (s)he was so young. Death came too soon." What age is too soon: 18, 28, 38 or even 88? Is not each of these ages too soon to die? You may say, "Well, I am a Christian. I believe in Christ, and Christ has promised life to all who believe in him!" True, but you're still going to die!

❀   ❀   ❀

Today would be a good day to die since you are thinking about death. Thinking about it, death wouldn't come as a thief to pickpocket you of life. Do you believe in your resurrection?

81

Do you believe in the promise of life given by Jesus to his followers, or do you only hope that it is true?

If today you had to meet, face-to-face, the flesh-eating beast at the center of the maze, could you die without regrets?

❁   ❁   ❁

FIFTH TUESDAY IN LENT

There was in the early church a haunting question of faith that Jesus' words about being the Resurrection *really* meant life after death for all who believe. To answer that doubt, John's Gospel account of the raising of Lazarus from the tomb in the Bethany cemetery was written sometime around the year 90 A.D. The sister of Lazarus, Martha, voiced the feelings of the young Christian community: "Lord, if you had been here, these people wouldn't be dying. You promised that if anyone was alive and believed in you they would never die. And now they're dying!" (See Jn. 11: 21, 25-26). Most of the contemporaries of Jesus had died already. What had happened to the promise?

Most of us would echo that question. What is the mixture of faith and hope in your belief about sharing in the Resurrection of Christ? Do you really believe, or do you merely *hope* that there's life after death? Regardless of your answer, this week you are invited to enter a two week Course in Dying.

If you choose not to become a student in such a course, you can spend these last two weeks saying prayers and being penitential. But if you'd like to commit to that course of study, begin today to look honestly at your own personal victory—like that of the Greek hero Theseus—over death.

As with other training courses, this one has special student clothing. The feast of Easter, only two weeks away, certainly is a festival of clothing. Recall that classic Irving Berlin song: *Put on your Easter bonnet, with all the frills upon it. You'll be the grandest lady in the Easter parade.* The feast of Easter is truly a time for special clothes!

Lent, likewise, has its special clothing: "Put on your sackcloth and ashes...." Four weeks ago you could have sung those words to the same Irving Berlin melody. Of course, neither you nor anyone else I know actually put on sackcloth shirts or gunnysack underwear. As for ashes, we had a few sprinkles on the forehead, and that was only on Ash Wednesday.

Sackcloth in the ancient world was used to make feed bags. Being the lowest grade of fabric, it was made into funeral attire. When your father, mother, spouse or friend died, you put on gunnysack and sprinkled ashes all over yourself as a sign of mourning. Sackcloth was also the symbolic clothing worn in times of national disaster, when the land was struck by some plague or overrun in war. The garment is mentioned frequently in the First or Old Testament and also in the Second Testament by Jesus. Consider today what might have happened if you had worn itchy burlap for the past four weeks? I assure you, you would not have forgotten that it is Lent.

❀   ❀   ❀

Not having worn sackcloth daily for the past four weeks, have you at times forgotten the purpose of these forty days? While you have read these daily reflections, perhaps prayed more than usual and maybe even fasted, has this Lent been more of a hobby than a true period of reform?

If you wish today that you could have invested yourself more in a true reform, take heart; it's not too late. Pledge to spend yourself with zeal in this Course in Dying—so that you can truly rejoice in the alleluia joy of Easter.

❀   ❀   ❀

FIFTH WEDNESDAY IN LENT

For the next two weeks of this training course, you could wear special clothing to remind you that you are a student. As a trainee in this course of study, you could wear not a hair shirt but a training shirt.

Shirts were originally worn by both men *and* women. They were very long garments that sometimes extended to the knees, sometimes to the floor. Recall pictures you may have seen of old-fashioned night shirts. These original shirts were gathered at the waist with a cord, and then an outer garment was worn over them.

Undershirts were first worn in the seventeenth century, and it was in 1940 that T-shirts appeared. T-shirts, which are so popular today, came from the Second World War. The "T" of T-shirts stood for training shirts which were worn by recruits in boot camp.

So, as a student in this Course in Dying, to assist you in remembering the importance of these days, you could wear a particular T- (training) shirt. Unfortunately they are not often available in the spring of the year, but inexpensive costumes of skeletons abound at Halloween. A training shirt could be made out of one of these costumes by simply cutting off the legs and arms. While the black T-shirt with white skeleton bones on the chest might seem grim and ugly, images like it are seen by some as beautiful art.

Sixteenth century Zen artists often used skeletons, skulls and dead flowers as subjects for their art. That choice flowed from a Buddhist concept which is also very Christian. The confrontation with death in Zen art is very Jesus-like because it proclaims that by honestly confronting and embracing the fleeting nature of life you can truly be alive. The Zen painters' skeletons, often pictured as grinning and dancing, are like X-ray photos of Fred Astaire dancing. They are reminiscent of the image of Christ dancing on the cross, from the painting in a cathedral in the south of France.

This two week Course in Dying is important since our culture's way of dealing with death is one of enormous denial. The psychologist author Rollo May addressed this denial over thirty years ago in *Love and Will*:

> The awareness of death is widely repressed in our day. But none of us can fail to be aware at the same time of the tremendous preoccupation with sex, in our humor, our drama, our economic life, even down to the commercials on television. An obsession drains off anxiety from some other

area and prevents the person from having to confront something distasteful. What would we have to see if we could cut through our obsession with sex? That we must die. The clamor of sex about us drowns out the ever waiting presence of death.

❋   ❋   ❋

Today's reflection on the denial of death prompts a personal question: how do you deny your own death, or the deaths of those you love and depend upon? Consider how you would treat those loved ones and their little quirks if you thought death were suddenly to take them from your life.

Reflect on whether your denial of death prevents you from being reconciled with those you find difficult. Before this day concludes, take time, at least in your heart, to be reconciled with all.

❋   ❋   ❋

FIFTH THURSDAY IN LENT

Today's obsession with health foods and dieting, excessive concerns about cholesterol and undo emphasis on physical exercise can be a way of denying death. True, a good healthy diet and plenty of exercise is important in helping us live a full life—and is certainly more wholesome than cosmetics or surgery as a way of staying young. But ask yourself: how much of it is an obsession? When it becomes the focal point of our lives, when no day can pass without it, then it can easily be another form of denial.

Death is a reality that each of us must face. It is a reality that must be faced with faith. Yes, you are going to die, but if you believe that you're really not going to perish when you die, then you can be like one of those Zen dancing skeletons. In the act of dancing with death, you can be enlightened.

Enlightenment is one of the goals of the spiritual life. It's like a 100 watt light bulb. If you inserted a brand new one into an electrical socket, its life expectancy would be 750 hours. The big light bulb, the big heat lamp in the sky, the sun, is going to burn out in five billion years! It won't simply go out like your light bulb, but rather, in a giant explosion, the sun will be blown into bits outward into space.

The water pump on your car has a three or four year life expectancy. So don't become upset when your water pump goes out in a couple of years. Is it supposed to last forever? Your life expectancy is about 28,000 days, approximately seventy-five years. At the time of Jesus, the average person had a life expectancy of only about thirty-five years. Barring all accidents, with the most amazing immune system in the world, the best you can expect is 115 years. If you're happy and stress free, you might hope to approach that maximum.

Trauma of various sorts, on the other hand, is bad for longevity. If you're divorced, have lost your spouse or are single, your life expectancy is greatly reduced. That just proves the wisdom of God's statement in Eden: "It's not good for Adam to be alone—he's not going to last very long." Yet, regardless of your age, whether you're very young or elderly, regardless of your health or marital status, at this moment the Beast, Death, is nibbling on you. That's what we need to confront.

❀   ❀   ❀

Reflect today not only on the length of life you desire but on the quality of life. To live many years can be a curse, especially if at this moment you are lonely and unhappy.

Aware that science may extend your life span beyond what you think is possible, what radical changes, what forms of Lenten remodeling, are required in your life to make today full of life? Don't delay in making those alterations. If you were able to make only one change in your life, what would you choose? Lastly, look at why you're delaying in making that change.

❀   ❀   ❀

FIFTH FRIDAY IN LENT

At this moment, as you read this Friday reflection, the Beast of Death is nibbling on you! Don't delay in your work of Lenten reform. Consider your sense of taste. It's at its height at age four or five! By the time you reach ten, you've lost thousands of taste buds. Around the age of thirty-five, you have only about 245 of them left. By the time you reach the age of eighty, only about eighty-eight taste buds remain. You forget—since Nature's kind to us—how good things used to taste when you were a child.

Your eyes, which you are now using to read this page, reach their peak when you're about seventeen and then start to decline. Your eye muscles begin to harden so that by the age of thirty or forty, you can't see as well. It's much worse at seventy, and if you live long enough, you'll go blind. There's no way to keep your eyesight forever.

Your sense of hearing is excellent around the age of ten. By forty, you're not hearing the rich overtones in music. By sixty you can't hear the upper notes of the robin's song. At eighty you're missing the best of fine music.

Your skin is in good shape until about twenty-five or thirty; after that it begins to fail. Wrinkles and creases appear around the eyes, and at forty-five or fifty bags begin to take shape under your eyes. By seventy you lose so much fat and water in the skin, which means your skin can't reflect ordinary light, that the skin absorbs the yellowness in the light and you begin to look pale and deathly.

Your bones, all two hundred of them, stop growing around twenty-five, and from then on they start shrinking. You're at your tallest at about twenty-five. Around forty, the Beast is busy compressing the discs in your spine, and your arches start falling. You start to become shorter and shorter and are bent over.

At this point, you're probably eager to say, "Stop! Enough of this!" Well, I told you it's boot camp, a special and particularly painful kind of boot camp since here

Truth is the name of your drill sergeant. I could guess that you're *dying* to ask, "Doesn't science have some good news?" Well, there is a partial reprieve, if you can watch the old odometer into the early part of the twenty-first century.

If you're alive in 2005, you probably won't have to worry about being bald. There will be a gene therapy transplant, and everyone can have hair. By 2010 science will be able to replace sense organs, which might be better than the originals. By 2012 it's highly possible there will be effective transplanting of limbs and internal organs. In about 2025 to 2050, life expectancy could be pushed to about 150 to 200 years. All this "good news" that you'll have these spare parts within you and that your life span will be extended is pretty impressive. Yet is it really good news?

The good news that you're looking for is the good news that Jesus didn't come to resuscitate dead bodies, as with Lazarus, or to extend life another fifty or sixty years. He came to teach us how to transform our lives, whatever amount is given to us. He came to show us how to rise above the pains and sufferings of daily life by a realization that we are already so alive that death itself cannot rob us of Life. Jesus invited us to join ourselves to him, the Ever-Living One, and to experience eternal life now in this life.

❀   ❀   ❀

Remember those holy pictures of early saints who kept a skull on their desk to remind them of death? That same reminder—the purpose of which was to confront death so as to be more alive—is available to you (at least if you're over thirty) by simply looking down at your hands! If you are wearing glasses to read this page, that's a reminder. Simply looking with honesty into the mirror can be a Lenten experience.

We're but one week away from Good Friday. Today is a good day to think about your own personal Good Friday, the day of your death. You should prepare for such an important day—more important than your birthday, your wedding day or ordination day—with great anticipation and care. If that seems distasteful, ask yourself why it seems so horrible a thought?

❀　　❀　　❀

FIFTH SATURDAY IN LENT

To believe that you will live beyond your death is a radical challenge, but a challenge of freedom. To live that belief daily is to be free of the great lie: "I'm not growing older." It's freedom from the grief of gray hair and wrinkles, whether at an early appearance in your thirties or their deepening in your eighties. Such a belief allows you to enter the parade. To paraphrase Irving Berlin: *Put on your holy T-shirt with all the bones a'dancin'. You'll be the grandest person in the Easter parade.*

That's a gift of faith: to believe that at this very moment you're in the Easter parade. The fifth Saturday in Lent, or any day, is a good time for the Easter parade down Fifth Avenue or the street on which you live. At times, the Easter parade also appears to be your own funeral procession since at the center of the Lenten labyrinth is not only

91

the rose but also the flesh-eating Beast. Yet look again at the famous labyrinth of the Cathedral of Chartres. Look at the rose in its center. That rose is like a rose window doorway through which you pass into a life that is filled with life, this life and Life beyond this life.

The author Thomas Moore says, "The body is the soul presented in its richest and most expressive form." You and I, all of us, are the words of God made flesh. The Spirit is enfleshed in us. Look then at your body not as an image of death and decay. Look through the rose window doorway which allows you to see your body as a manifestation of your soul.

In today's culture, soul doesn't often enter into our consciousness about exercise or diet, not to mention our daily work and activities. It's more common for us to think about ourselves as machines. The purpose of life in today's society seems to be to keep the machine running as efficiently as possible for as long as possible. Indeed, you and I need to be concerned about our food, our exercise and our daily activities and pursuits, but whatever we eat or do, let it be done soulfully.

The separation today of life and religion, of everyday life and "soul times," would have been incomprehensible in the culture of Jesus. For Jesus and his contemporaries, soul, body and mind were inseparable. Together they were a seamless reality. What divided them was Greek philosophy. You and I live cursed by that split.

One result is the human body being regarded like an automobile. Fast food places are just like gasoline stations: we feed the body as if we were filling the gas tank. It's ironic, if not symbolic, that most gasoline stations today also sell fast food! Fill your tank and your stomach in one stop, and just as fast.

Is it possible to imagine taking two hours to fill your gasoline tank? You are not a machine; you have a soul. When you eat in a leisurely way, you feed the soul. If you exercise, do so in a way that involves both body and soul.

❀ ❀ ❀

A Saturday boot camp assignment is to make meals into times for soul food. A similar Course in Dying assignment would be to say "body" each time you say "soul." And every time you say "soul," say "body." See them as twin words.

One week from today is Holy Saturday. Practice, then, in the week that remains, saying, "Boy, does my back—and soul—hurt." What affects the soul usually afflicts the body. Create a new personal vocabulary of Body-Soul so that when you get to the center of the maze and see the Beast, you can smile, for you will see as well the rose of the resurrection.

Recall the words of Paul to the Romans:

If the Spirit of the One who raised Jesus from the dead dwells in you, then the One who raised Christ from the dead will bring your mortal bodies to life also through the Spirit dwelling within you (Rm. 8: 10-11).

❀ ❀ ❀

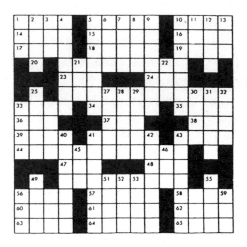

PASSION OR PALM SUNDAY

Prayerfully recall the story of the first palm parade as found in the Gospel of Matthew:

As they drew near Jerusalem, entering Bethphage on the Mount of Olives, Jesus sent off two of his disciples, telling them: "Go into the village straight ahead and you will immediately find an ass tethered and her colt with her. Untie them and bring them back to me. If anyone says anything, say to them, 'The Master needs them.' Then he will let them go at once." All this was to fulfill the words of the prophet: "Tell the daughter of Zion, your king comes to you without display astride an ass, astride a colt, the foal of a beast of burden."

The disciples did what Jesus asked; they brought him the ass and the colt and laid their cloaks on them, and he mounted. The huge crowd spread their cloaks on the road, while some began to cut branches from the trees and laid them along his path. The groups preceding as well as those who followed kept crying out: "God save the Son of David! Blessed is he who comes in the name of the Lord! God save him from on high!"

As Jesus entered Jerusalem, the whole city, stirred to its depths, demanded, "Who is this?" And the crowd with Jesus kept answering, "This is the prophet Jesus from Nazareth in Galilee" (Mt. 21: 1-11).

Today, to the ancient echoes of the crowd's jubilant shouts during that first palm parade, you have finally reached the inner circle of the Lenten labyrinth. As you cross over into the very core of the maze, you will enter the mystery of the cross and into the shrine of Holy Week. You have come to the conclusion of another Lent, this time with its journey through the labyrinth.

When you began on the first Sunday of Lent, if you recall, it was proposed that the publishers of parish missalettes should put puzzles on their covers! It was suggested that such covers might be more productive for people than the usual religious art or prayers. Waiting for Mass to begin, or during boring sermons, people could spend their idle time working on the puzzles.

The puzzle for this last Sunday is a unique one, a crossword puzzle! Such a puzzle is appropriate for this feast. You might say, "Appropriate? A crossword puzzle seems terribly inappropriate for Palm Sunday!" To help us understand how a crossword puzzle might be more fitting for this Palm Sunday than some traditional design, a brief review of the history of word puzzles may be of assistance.

Crossword puzzles are an American invention, first appearing in 1913 in *The New York World*. At that time they were called Word Crosses. In a brief eleven years time, they had become the rage in America. Pollsters found that by 1924, 60% of Americans traveling on trains spent their time working crossword puzzles. They were such a national craze that the B&O Railroad placed dictionaries in all its cars, and the Pennsylvania Railroad even printed crossword puzzles on the back of the menus in its dining cars. Dictionaries to help solve these puzzles were in such demand that some librarians were forced to post limits of five minutes on their use.

When news of this American fad crossed the Atlantic, the British were horrified. *The London Times* called it "Shameful and disgracing..." that America was so enslaved. The *Times* stated that, "Daily over five million hours of work is lost by employees doing crossword puzzles at work." However, like other things American, it wasn't long before crossword puzzles became the craze in England. They were so popular that during the Second World War the Nazis dropped propaganda leaflets on England in the form of crossword puzzles. One such propaganda puzzle called for a nine-letter word for warmonger. The answer turned out to be "Churchill."

Skill and patience are required to compose a crossword puzzle and to edit it carefully to be free of errors. Most of the time, they are flawless. A notable exception is a classic error which appeared in *The New York Times*. The puzzle asked for a four-letter word for a Catholic chief. When the answer was printed the next day, it caused an uproar. The editor was bombarded with telephone calls because of one simple letter. The answer was printed as "Dope"! The editor frantically assured everyone that it was an error and not an act of religious discrimination.

In 1959 Gallup Polls revealed that the crossword puzzle was the number one game for Americans, surpassing poker, bridge, chess and checkers. Crosswords have slipped in popularity today, however, because television makes them seem too slow paced, too dull. Furthermore, much of today's generation finds words themselves or reading a newspaper to be puzzling, and many would be lost *with* dictionaries.

Crossword puzzles are a lot like religion, which also can be boring. An official of the Vatican, Archbishop Foley, the head of the Commission for Communications, recently said, "Communicating our faith is a compelling matter. In modern communication the greatest sin is to be dull." A novel mortal sin, then, would be a dull Palm Sunday liturgy.

Palm Sunday, if it isn't dull, certainly is a puzzlement: Jesus riding serenely up to Jerusalem, while the crowds proclaim him to be the Messiah, the king. It's a puzzle because Jesus previously had rejected the title of king. So why did he allow the palm procession to happen? What was the meaning of his riding *serenely* up to Jerusalem? Had he not told his disciples, "I will go up to Jerusalem where wicked men will insult me and crucify me"? While such a death was a painful puzzlement to the disciples, Jesus' triumphant entrance into Jerusalem was not. The disciples rejoiced in the roar of the crowd, rejoiced that finally Jesus had acknowledged publicly who he truly was.

We know that God's inspiration is not restricted to the First and Second Testaments. Whenever and wherever in the other holy books you find the truth, you know that the Spirit of God is its author. Centuries before Christ, in ancient China, the *Tao Te Ching* was written. Chapter 16 reads:

> Each being in the universe
>   returns to the common source.
> Returning is the source of serenity.
> When you realize where you come from,
>   you naturally become disinterested, amused,
>   kindhearted as a grandmother,
>   dignified as a king.
> Immersed in the wonder of the Tao, the way,
>   you can deal with whatever life brings you.
> And when death comes, you are ready.

Jesus, then, gentle-hearted as a grandmother, as dignified as a king, could ride serenely up to his death because he *knew* he was returning to his source. He knew he would mount not a royal throne but a rugged cross. He knew that not a crown of jewels but a crown of thorns would go on his head. That's what life had brought him, and he accepted it with serenity because he knew where he had come from and where he was going.

❀　　❀　　❀

On this first Sunday inside the inner-circle of the labyrinth, ask yourself if you can go to your death with serenity. Can you view death, or even the present stage of your aging process, as a return to the source from which you have come?

Presently, how are you dealing with what life has brought to you? When you reject the hand you are dealt in life and want better cards with which to play the game of life, you will most likely rage against your death. This last stage of Lent begins just as the season of Lent itself began: by a reflection on your death. Today is a good day to die.

❀   ❀   ❀

MONDAY OF HOLY WEEK

Those who reject the fact that the puzzle of existence, the labyrinthian way of life, leads directly to death are not serene. They typically become rebels who war against aging. They rage against pain. They struggle against and deny their demise. Pain, suffering and death are all part of the path. Those who rebel against the reality of that way, are reduced to using drugs, alcohol and tranquilizers. The drugs they use include work, TV, sex and endless amusements—anything to kill the rage and the pain within them.

However, if you are immersed in the wonder of the way, you can deal with whatever life brings you. The way of Christ when practiced as a religion is usually dull. The way of Christ, however, when seen as a labyrinthian maze, causes one to be immersed in wonder. The question is: how does one achieve this baptism in wonder? Perhaps this is where we need to return to the crossword puzzle as the appropriate sacred symbol for Palm Sunday.

Crossword puzzles, by definition, are crosses composed of words. Words can be nouns, verbs, adverbs and adjectives. A noun, from the Latin *nomen*, refers to an object, such as a tree, house or desk. Nouns are static realities. A verb, however, from the Latin *verbum*, is active, as in running, seeing or praying.

If you were working a crossword puzzle which required a nine-letter word for a disciple of Christ, you would probably choose a noun such as "Christian." The grammar rules for a Palm Sunday crossword puzzle, however, say that instead of a nine-letter noun, the correct answer would be an unheard-of eleven-letter verb, "Christianing." The "ing" added to the end makes it into something active and dynamic.

It is true not only of Jesus: You and I also are words of God made flesh. Each person, each creature, is a unique word of God made flesh. Whenever you use a noun to define yourself, like "Christian," it implies that you are a completed project instead of being in process. You could be a verb, but most people prefer to be nouns. It's less work since you can be static, whether you're defining yourself as a husband, wife or mother. If you wish to be immersed in wonder, search for ways to change your self-definition from noun terms to a rich variety of active verb images.

A story may help clarify the need to become a verb. It's from a book called *Travels in Small Towns in America* by Bill Bryson. He tells about going to Hannibal, Missouri to visit the home of Mark Twain, which is located in the center of the downtown district. The city charges guests two dollars to tour Mark Twain's boyhood home. You cannot enter it, but you can look in through the windows. At each window there is a button with a recorded message which speaks about the room.

100

Bryson tells about how disappointed he was since it was supposed to be a faithful reproduction of the home of Mark Twain. In the bedroom, however, there was Armstrong vinyl on the floor, and there were a lot of other things that just didn't fit. As he was walking around the house, he met a friendly stranger of whom he inquired, "May I ask, what do you think of the house?"

The man said, "It's wonderful. Every time I come to Hannibal, which is two or three times a year, I always come here. In fact, even if I'm just nearby, I try to make it here to see Mark Twain's house. I've probably been here twenty-five or thirty times."

Bryson was amazed and he said, "Really! Can I ask you one more question, then? Do you think the house is authentic, I mean the way Mark Twain spoke about it in his books?" The stranger said, "Well, sir, I really don't know. You see, I've never read any of his books. But this is a real shrine!"

❀　　❀　　❀

On this Monday in Holy Week, reflect on the fact that you can come to the mystery of this holiest of weeks as did the visitor to Mark Twain's house—as to a shrine. It can be wonderful, dramatic and impressive, yet you may never have heard or read a word that Jesus spoke, never really entered into Christ's life.

Read slowly this small part of the Letter to the Philippians. As you read, let the words ask you questions about how you view death. Let these words sink deeply into your soul as you ponder your attitude and that of Christ:

> *Your attitude must be Christ's:*
> *though he was in the form of God,*
> 　*he did not deem equality with God*

as something to be grasped at.
Rather he emptied himself
and took the form of a slave,
being born in human likeness...
he humbled himself,
obediently accepting even death,
death on a cross (Phil. 2: 6-8).

❋   ❋   ❋

TUESDAY OF HOLY WEEK

Early in the Lenten journey we hear the harsh require-
ments of Jesus for those who wish to join the way, "If you
wish to be my disciple, you must deny your very self, take
up your cross and follow me" (Mt. 17: 24). Contained in
those words is the secret of how to change a noun into a
verb. Whenever your life is *crisscrossed* with pain and
suffering, with sickness, divorce or any one of a number
of problems, then something static can become something dynamic. The nouns, Jim or Mary, when crisscrossed with cancer or a catastrophe suddenly become
dynamic active agents.

"Take up your cross"; what does that mean? In the
Gospel of Luke it seems very evident. Crosses were for
revolutionaries. They were the instruments of capital
punishment for anyone who opposed Rome, who worked
actively against the establishment to lift the oppression of

the people. All crosses can be revolutionary, socially renewing as they help to redeem—to make holy—the world. Jesus the Galilean would have remained just Jesus the Galilean without his cross. It was the cross that made him Christ. You and I, without our crosses, remain simply Catholics, Methodists or Lutherans. The cross is what makes you a "Christianing," a dynamic disciple.

For two millenniums, the question has been asked: does being a disciple of Christ imply a vocation to social revolution and social change? You may ask, "Is that the cross I'm supposed to pick up and carry?" Before you answer that question, look again at the crossword puzzle design at the top of the Palm Sunday reflection. At its center are *two* crosses! It suggests that as a disciple you may be required to carry more than one cross! Besides the revolutionary cross of Christ, you also have a cross of personal revolution and transformation. You are to carry it as well, lest it crush and destroy you.

Another term for "to puzzle" is "to mystify," which implies that the meaning is hidden. When you take up your crosses, you begin the sacred alchemy not of mystified transformation but of mystical transformation. The transformation achieved by embracing your crosses is not just puzzling, it is prayerful as well. It inextricably unites you and the world.

Moreover, the cross and the palm should be perpetual companions. If you were given a crossword question, "What is a seven-letter word for palm?" the correct answer would be: V-i-c-t-o-r-y. The palm branch was the instrument of victory given to the gladiators in the arena and the symbol of victory carried by the martyrs in the apocalyptic visions of St. John. When you pick up your crosses and carry them, it is victorious for you and the world.

There is story of a professional soccer player in Madrid, whose life was playing soccer. He was presented with a cross of transformation in the form of a car accident which paralyzed him from the waist down for a year and a half. The accident destroyed his career as a professional soccer player and devastated him. During his rehabilitation a sympathetic nurse brought him a guitar in the hospital. While he didn't have any particular musical aspirations, he began playing the guitar and singing. His creative chemistry with his cross made Julio Iglesias an international celebrity who has gifted the world with the beauty of his music.

Julio Iglesias didn't sink into victimhood and cry, "Poor me! Paralyzed in a car accident." The palm branches of this Holy Week symbolize the process of how victimhood can become priesthood. Priests offer sacrifice, *sacra facere*, "to make holy." Whatever affliction comes to you in your journey of life can be a melodramatic mystery or a blessed bafflement. When you walk in the wonder of the way and come to the center of the labyrinth, as in the crossword puzzle, you find two crosses.

One of them is the cross of Jesus the Galilean, the model for how we should embrace ours. Next to it is your personal cross. While you may be mystified, baffled, puzzled by it, you need to embrace it with a sense of peace—and with patience.

❀   ❀   ❀

Here are two Holy Week reflections for this day. The first is: how well are you carrying the cross of Christ? Does the work of bringing justice and peace to the world, of redeeming it, fit your shoulders? How involved are you in the sufferings of the poor, society's weak and little ones who lack power?

The second reflection is: whatever your personal cross or crosses, are you engaged in the creative chemistry of converting them into something that will enhance you and the world? Has your personal cross ordained you to victimhood or priesthood?

❀　❀　❀

WEDNESDAY OF HOLY WEEK

Today you stand in the inner circle of the labyrinth, halfway between last Sunday's victory parade and the Easter parade of this coming Sunday's feast of the Resurrection of Christ. Some Christians prefer to take a short cut in the Lenten labyrinth and go directly from the victory parade of palms to the alleluia victory of Easter. If you desire to taste the rare vintage of Easter joy, however, do not take the short cut!

Walk faithfully with Christ in the mysteries of this week, for they are a mirror of the maze of life itself. In such a journey of pain, suffering and ultimate victory there are no short cuts. The journey of the labyrinth's inner-circle, the seven days of Holy Week, contains conflicting and complex experiences. It includes the memory of the praise and the palms at the victorious entrance into Jerusalem, the sharing of a friendship meal of love, the betrayal of friends, especially the great betrayal of one of the chosen twelve. It reaches its crossroads in the puzzle of the shame and pain of the crucifixion as an expression of the will of a loving God for a beloved son. Then it leads you to the despair and emptiness of the grave and the final defeat of the one who said he was the Life of the world.

The puzzle of such conflicting emotions, with the ugliness of a painful death and the bitter taste of defeat explains why so many prefer to take the short cut from Palm Sunday to Easter. How can you seek a resolution to that puzzle and the puzzlement of your personal crosses in life?

When working a crossword puzzle, sometimes it seems impossible to find the correct word for the number of spaces allowed. You may have searched the dictionary and racked your brain without success. Another strategy is to solve the difficult question by solving the other words around it. As certain letters line up on either side of the blank spaces, the puzzle begins to solve itself. So it is with our problems.

Your cross in life may be a mystery that seems to escape understanding. If you begin to daily solve the little puzzles around the big one, slowly the large mystery will resolve itself. This is what it means to "take up your cross," to embrace the reality of your life as the mysterious way God has chosen for you. As with an embrace between friends, your cross should be embraced wholeheartedly. It should be embraced without reservation, without pity, without regret. You embrace it because your cross, like the cross of Jesus, is the means by which you become holy—and by which the world becomes holy.

The palm branch you received last Sunday can be of assistance in your efforts to transform your crosses into

106

agents of reform. As a powerful symbol of victory, it can remind you of how the cross is a vehicle of victory. Remember that it is a branch from a palm tree just as your cross is a branch on the tree of Christ's cross. Your cross is thus a part of God's redemptive mystery of the world, which is truly a mystery of sharing with Christ in his divine vocation.

❀   ❀   ❀

Here are a few ways for using your palm branch as a prayerful reminder of how your personal cross is a branch on the cross of Christ. You could take a small piece of your palm and tuck it in your wheel chair, if you use one. You could wrap it around your wedding ring if you're in a troubled marriage.

You could place a piece of your palm in your billfold if you're having financial problems. A piece of palm could be worn on your undershirt over your heart if you're brokenhearted, or it could be placed next to your medicine jar or prescription bottle if you're ill or dying from cancer or AIDS. You could insert it into the frame of a photograph of a son or a daughter who is having problems.

The palm possibilities are as numerous as are life's crosses. Especially in these sacred days of Holy Week, use your palm branch, or pieces of it, to awaken yourself to the victory inherent in embracing your cross.

❀   ❀   ❀

HOLY THURSDAY

On this fifth day of Holy Week, as you pass through the labyrinth's inner circle, you are blocked by a table which is set for a feast. The dining table blocks your passage, and you must confront its meaning here at the center of the maze and its significance in the midst of these holy days.

Christians for almost two thousand years have celebrated, not only on this feast, but each week and even daily, the memorial meal of the Last Supper of Jesus with his disciples. His first disciples called it the "Lord's Supper," the "Breaking of the Bread" and the "Agape." In the first century it was called the "Eucharist," Greek for "thanksgiving."

The Greek word *Agape* means "love," the magnet that drew Jesus to the heart of the great labyrinth of his death and Resurrection—the same magnet that has drawn you daily deeper and deeper into this maze. On the night before his death, at that last meal with his friends, Jesus spoke with great passion of his love for them and for the world.

Love, Jesus said, would be at the heart of the community of his companions, the new family that he was creating. By washing his disciples' feet at that meal, he revealed how to recognize a great lover. The greater the love, the greater the desire to be of service, even in the most humble of actions. Also, Jesus said, loving, humble service is the most powerful cure for the deadly virus of power and prestige.

None of the Gospel accounts of the final meal mention the lamb, crucial for a seder meal. Bread and wine are the focus of this menu. Scholars conjecture that the institution of the Eucharist probably occurred not at a Passover meal but at a friendship meal. Common at that time, friendship meals were table gatherings of friends who had come together for devotional purposes, for some common cause or simply to share in friendship. At the same time, these Jewish friendship meals held an echo of the Passover meal which was the greatest event in their history, just as Christians today reverence every meal as an echo of the Last Supper.

Friendship meals were celebrated by disciples with their teacher. They were warm, intimate times of friends sharing stories and their lives. At such a meal the teacher Jesus desired to teach his greatest lesson on love, and he did something very inventive. He creatively turned the traditional *berakhot* prayers, the blessing prayers for a meal, into a new ritual for transformation. To the orthodox prayer of the blessing of bread, he added, "This is my body." To the table prayer for wine, he added, "This is my blood poured forth in love for you and for all the world. Do this in memory of me" (See Mk. 14: 22-25).

Then Jesus added a message to his disciples, "Love one

another. Such as my love has been for you, so must your love be for each other. The command I give you is to love one another" (See Jn. 15: 12, 17). With these words on love at his final friendship meal, the Teacher supplied the most essential ingredient for curing the terminal illness of the world. He also shared the secret of the source of the courage and strength to bear one's cross, a deep and passionate love. Love has been the power that has brought you this far on your Lenten journey, and only a great love of God and self will energize you to continue on the dark and deadly crooked path ahead.

Love is a word that evokes images of great affection, but to those of the Near Eastern world of Jesus it had less a connotation of passionate affection than of *attachment*. To love God with all your heart, mind and body was to be totally attached to God—and to God's design for the perfection of the world. To love Jesus is to be likewise attached to him and his vision of the new Reign of God, a global community of unity, peace and justice. To love one another means being attached—with great depth and devotion—to your brothers and sisters of the family of Christ. It implies that your attachment to their needs must be as great as your attachment to your own needs.

The paradox of life's labyrinthian journey is that while it is uniquely personal, it is also a corporate journey. We never walk alone, we never save our own soul without also saving the world. The Jewish Passover meal was linked to the Lord's Supper, scholars propose, so that it could become the Christian Passover. The seder meal was a *family* meal. In the Book of Exodus God said to Moses: "Tell the whole community of Israel...every one of your families must procure for itself a lamb, one apiece for each household. If a family is too small for a whole lamb, it shall join the nearest household in procuring one" (Ex. 12: 3-4). The "Do-This-in-Memory-of-Me" meal of Christ was to be more than a friendship meal. It was meant to be a family feast, an extended family that would be global.

The love feast of the disciples became the memorial meal of the new family of Jesus which is composed not of people related by blood or neighborhood but by faith. This family's members were to commit themselves to carry on and live out the message of Jesus and to be loyal to God's dream of a new world. By sharing a memory meal, a living memory of Christ's death and Resurrection, the vision would be handed on. That memory of Christ's actions at the Last Supper, like our DNA code, was imprinted with God's design for the healing and restoration of the world: loving until death.

This reflection on Holy Thursday concludes with the toast Jesus gave at the end of his last dinner. He said to his friends, "I tell you, I will not drink this fruit of the vine from now until the day when I drink it new with you in my Father's Kingdom" (Mt. 26: 29). That's the toast which holds the promise of Easter morning. It is a proclamation that love is stronger than death. Perhaps whenever we share a glass of wine with those we love, we should raise the glass up high and propose this toast, "Until we drink this again, forever new in the Kingdom!"

❋　　❋　　❋

As you pray on this Thursday in Holy Week, consciously unite yourself with Christ's global family. Experience your heart expanding outward to love—to be attached—to all that God has created, the whole body of Christ. As you prayerfully remember the various needs of your brothers and sisters, known and unknown, strive to be as attached to their needs as you are to your own needs.

Pray for an increase of love in your heart over the journey of the final two days of the Lenten pilgrimage. Ask God for the gift of zeal, that flaming passion not fueled by hormones or pleasant feelings. As a gift of the Spirit of the Holy, zeal is essential if you are to carry your cross up the crooked path to Calvary, California, Texas or Ohio—wherever your personal Mount Calvary is located.

Today, if possible, attend a celebration of the Lord's Last Supper, the Eucharist of Holy Thursday, with your parish community or church. Make your principal meal today as festive as possible since Holy Thursday is the feast day of all dinners. With family and any friends present, you can give the Last Supper toast, "Until we drink this again, forever new in the Kingdom."

At your home or church celebration of today's feast, even if you live alone, place a chair or several chairs at your table to symbolically seat members of your global family in Christ. Acknowledge their mystical presence at your table. Also acknowledge silently to yourself that your work of reform and prayer this Lenten season has been done as part of a global effort. Your Lenten work has graced the hearts of others who in turn have helped build up the body of Christ.

❀　　❀　　❀

GOOD FRIDAY

Perhaps no other single death day has been the subject of so many sermons, works of art, books, songs, poems, films and theatrical plays as the one that you are contemplating this Friday. Still, the mystery of the shame and pain of that Black Friday has not yet been fully explored or explained, nor is it likely to be unraveled in another two thousand years. Good Friday's death of Jesus on the cross is veiled with countless unanswerable questions about God, about Jesus, about who was responsible for this crime and about its purpose in the plan of redemption.

Having departed from the warm, intimate friendship meal of Holy Thursday evening, you passed through the pale moonlit olive garden of the mental crucifixion of Jesus. There, like a child, he pleaded not to be subjected to what his father was asking of him. Being firmly attached to God and God's will, however, he embraced the bitter cup of his death—first through shame, and then in pain.

Your labyrinthian reflection for this Good Friday is

the parable Gospel of Bartimeaus, the once-blind beggar of Jericho. Let this gospel be a summary of your journey over these Lenten days, providing an insight into your daily labyrinthian journey. May it assist you in seeing behind the veil of the ancient mysteries of this Good Friday.

A reading from the Lost Gospel according to Saint Bartimeaus:

Rabboni had just healed me as he made his way up to Jerusalem for the feast of the Passover. The great crowd that accompanied him had tried to silence me, but I only cried out the louder: "Son of David, heal me." And he did! I tossed aside my blind beggar's cloak, the coins flying everywhere, and I followed him.

The crowds grew larger the closer we came to the Holy City. Some were pulling branches from palm trees; others gathered reeds from the fields. Rabboni's disciples were excited and kept shouting: "Now is the hour! This is the day the Lord has made!" Then Jesus ordered two of them to go ahead of us to Bethany and get a donkey. When they returned, he mounted it and rode in front of the throng toward the Golden Gate of the walled Holy City. I overheard some in the masses saying, "A donkey? Is that any way for the son of David, our glorious Messiah, to lead us in the great battle against the Romans?"

Jerusalem, the Holy City, was a great labyrinth with a thousand complicated passageways, baffling twists and turns of narrow streets. It was a maze more elaborate than the fabled labyrinths of

Egypt or Crete. A hopeless course for the blind, I wondered upon entering if we could ever find our way out again. We surged through the massive gate, pouring like a flooded river down the narrow street. Next to me in the crowd was Rebecca, whom Rabboni had cured of deafness. "Hear, Bartimaeus, the loud hosannas? Blessed is the kingdom of our father David to come, to come this very day."

"I hear, Rebecca, and I see the Zealots, the revolutionaries, with swords hidden in their cloaks. But look, up there on the rooftops: Roman soldiers everywhere."

Suddenly Jesus turned left down a street that led to the Fortress of Antonio, Gabbatha, Pilate's headquarters. The shouts of hosanna grew louder. The crowd became a mob, filled with hate and violence. At the end of the street in front of the fortress, however, Jesus turned right, down a twisting, narrow street. The rebels among us yelled, "Coward, fool, this is the day of the Lord! Strike now, the people are with us!" The Roman legions on the walls of the fortress only roared with laughter at the Jew on his donkey.

Rabboni, however, rode on in silence. A terrorist grabbed my arm: "He's betrayed us. He's afraid to restore the kingdom of David. Let's go home." But I saw. At each blank wall, Rabboni turned down another street till we came to the great Temple of Herod.

The Temple guards stood shoulder to shoulder across its entrance, the priests and scribes stood on the steps behind them. Rabboni rode up to them and thundered out, "My house is a house of prayer, but you have turned it into a den of thieves."

The Temple clergy shouted back, "Blasphemer! On whose authority do you speak?" The palm-waving crowd stood in awe at the drama unfolding before them and at the spectacle of the splendrous Temple. The golden plates on its side reflected the sun's radiance like mirrors. It shimmered like a star come to earth.

"See this Temple?" Jesus declared to the priests: "Not a stone will be left standing upon a stone. If you have faith, you can say to this mountain, 'Fly into the sea!' and it will plunge out of sight." Swiftly Jesus turned the donkey and headed down another passageway deeper into the maze.

"Where's he going?" cried someone in the crowd. But I saw and Rebecca heard.

"He's following the song," Rebecca shouted in my ear over the echoes of hosannas. "Do you hear?" My ears, keen from years of blindness, could make out the magnetic music.

As we descended deeper into the lane of the labyrinth, one of Rabboni's disciples pressed next to me, his palm branch broken in half. "What does he mean, 'God's house will be destroyed,' and 'My house shall be a house of prayer'? The Rabbi has no house, no family—he's childless!" I saw. We, this crowd of former beggars, of those once blind and deaf, former prostitutes, sinners and rejects— we who could "hear"—were his "house." Suddenly we exited from a twisted alley into a great square. A towering Gothic cathedral rose before us. Bishops and priests in scarlet vestments were processing into the cathedral to the fanfare of trumpets. The crowd, like ours, held palm branches, and robed choirs sang beautiful hosannas to the music of Handel's *Messiah*.

Rabboni's donkey stood still as he watched the ritual. Then he turned to us, saying, "Be constantly on the watch! Stay awake!" Cocking his head, he listened for a moment. Then he led us out of the square, down a dark, narrow lane. Rebecca cried out, "Do you hear it?"

"Yes, I hear." *Through many dangers, toils and snares I have already come. 'Tis grace that brought me safe thus far and grace will lead me home.*

As we plunged deeper into the maze of the garbage-littered alleyways, I saw expressions on the faces of Rabboni's apostles written large with disappointment. They had seen the scarlet robes, the awe with which the crowds held the cathedral's clergy, and they muttered to themselves, "Why did we not join them? Why did we have to come this way?" Some of those following the donkey and its silent, sad rider whispered, "He does not know where he's going; we'll never find our way out of this maze."

The singing of hosannas had grown faint. Palm branches, once waved in jubilation, now hung limp upon the shoulders of those remaining in the crowd. Overhead, a springtime storm was brewing; thunder rumbled as a blinding flash of lightning jabbed downward into the Holy City. Twisting and turning in the dim, smelly lanes, we passed the shacks of the poor. Jesus halted his donkey at the entrance of an open door, then shook his head and rode on. As I went past the doorway, I looked inside. An old woman in a black shawl knelt in the glow of vigil lights in front of statues of saints and the Virgin. She was burning a palm branch, praying, "Protect me from the evil eye and from the evil of this storm."

Suddenly we turned from the narrow lane into another great square filled with people. At one end was another cathedral. It was bedecked with flags, its bells joyfully ringing. From a nearby pen an oxen was driven out. It was frenzied because for days food and water had been placed within its sight but out of reach. Men, women and children with sticks, knives, whips and lances attacked the ox. At each exit it was driven back, as people gleefully struck the wild, bloody beast. Women threw pepper into its eyes as it ran crazed with pain in the midst of the attacking crowd. Rabboni rode straight through the wild crowd to the steps of the cathedral where a priest was sprinkling the people with holy water. "What is this madness?" Rabboni asked.

"This is our three day festival of Easter, stranger. This is *Farra de Boi*: the ox represents the Jew Judas who betrayed our blessed Lord. Here in the Brazilian state of Santa Catarina, over thirty villages hold to this blessed tradition. It will end two days from now when the ox is finally killed and butchered for a great feast. You and your friends, stay with us. Celebrate our blessed Lord's victory."

Jesus spurred his donkey forward, "What victory, for God's sake?"

Again we wandered this way and that through the Holy City's maze of narrow lanes till we came upon a wide curving street that led upward. "At last he's found a way out of this labyrinth," cried an apostle. But alas, after ascending the ramp we found ourselves on a four-lane freeway with cars bumper to bumper in the endless rush-hour traffic. Rabboni rode his donkey through the traffic as the crowd—what remained of it—tried to avoid being run down by the cars. Some drivers shook their fists and shouted in anger at our slowing down the flow, while others only smiled silly grins at us. Out of nowhere came sirens and flashing red lights, and two police cars herded us off the freeway. "All right, mister, get off the donkey. Who do you think you are? Didn't you see the sign at the entrance of the interstate? No animals, ridden or driven, slow-moving machinery or pedestrians allowed! Do you have a parade permit?"

"I'm only following the song," said Jesus as the police escorted us down the exit ramp.

Before us was a great complex, larger than the Temple and surrounded by hundreds of parked cars. Rabboni rode his donkey through the parking lot and into the shopping mall. We followed, awe-struck by the green trees and pools of water indoors, by the shops filled with wonders beyond imagination. The mall was jammed with people rushing in all directions. A haggard looking woman with several children in tow stopped Jesus: "Where's Penney's? I've got to get new Easter clothes for the kids." A couple with two small children asked him, "Do you know where in the mall is the big Easter Bunny that's giving away free Easter eggs?" Jesus only shook his head sadly and rode on. Then a security guard demanded of us: "Get your ass out of the mall!" So Jesus, with what was left of us who followed, rode out of an exit.

Again we were back in the maze of the Holy City, twisting and turning, but also, it seemed, ascending. On every side there were small shops selling religious articles: statues, crucifixes and bibles. Over the door of one store was a sign: **Relics of the True Cross. Holy Week Discount**. Rabboni rode on, his head hung in sorrow. Then he stopped, pointing toward one shop. It belonged to a woodworker. Its sign swayed in the wind: **Crosses for Sale**. Jesus turned to us, now only a ragged handful: "Go inside and choose one."

His shocked disciples replied, "Master, crosses are used only for those guilty of revolution, sedition against the Empire, those guilty of treason or robbery."

"I know! Don't you see?" They only shook their heads, blind to the meaning of his words, but I saw.

Rabboni slowly turned his head right and left, then spurred his donkey onward.

"Hear it, Bartimaeus?"

"Yes, Rebecca."

Faintly coming from somewhere ahead of us, the song went on: *For God has promised good to me. God's word my hope secures. God will my shield and portion be, as long as life endures.*

He rode onward and ever upward till we saw it. There in the center of the Holy City's great labyrinth was a hill scattered with sculls and bones. The apostles fled backward down the narrow lane. Jesus called after them, "No, come back! There's no other way through the maze. This is the only way out."

Dismounting the donkey, as black storm clouds swirled menacingly over the hilltop and sheets of rain lashed down, he turned his face upward full into the rain. The handful of us who were left stood over our broken palm branches dangling at our sides as he began to sing: *Amazing grace has banished fear and given life to me. I once was lost, but now I'm found, was blind, but now I see.*

❀   ❀   ❀

Reflect on whether, having come this deeply into the labyrinth, like Jesus, you realize that now there's only one way out. With whom in the parable gospel did you most identify: Bartimeaus? Rebecca? The disappointed disciples and Zealots? The drivers on the freeway? The Christ-figure?

Ask yourself if you are more drawn to the rich ceremonies or the superstitious powers of religious objects, to relics of the True Cross or to your true cross?

❀   ❀   ❀

HOLY SATURDAY
The Seventh Day of Holy Week

The labyrinth's path has spiraled sharply downward and has led you into a burial cave deep beneath the pavement of the maze. Unlike the previous twisting and turning pattern, today there is *no* path to follow. Your way is blocked as you stand before a stone wall. Rather than a wall, it's a giant stone rolled before a tomb which blocks your path. You have come to the tomb of Jesus, the dead wonder worker of Galilee.

Holy Saturday is an empty day, yet full of defeat. It is a day as hopeless as a barren womb, as void of promise as a desert wasteland. While being involved in activities preparing for tomorrow's feast of Easter, do your best to keep this day empty and hopeless. Strive to overcome your awareness of the historical fact—reinforced by two millenniums of tradition—about the Easter sunrise stories of the Resurrection. Because of that history, you will find it difficult to keep today empty of hope.

As you anticipate tomorrow, you will be aware that

Jesus did keep his promise about rising again. To prayerfully spend this day devoid of hope does not require play acting, only the ability to suspend history and time. If you live in the present moment of this day, Holy Saturday can provide you the same challenge it presented to the original disciples of Jesus, the challenge of clinging to the promise of eternal life in the face of death.

On the wings of imagination, travel in space and time to the various cemeteries and graveyards where those you love are buried. Visit each of their tombs, carrying not flowers but the promise of Christ that all who are one with him in love and faith shall rise from death. At each of their graves, proclaim your firm belief, and not simply a hope, that each of them also shall have a glorious Easter Sunday.

Pause and prayerfully remember all the holy dead whom you have known in life, especially those who have most touched your life. After each name in your personal litany, add the prayerful proclamation, "Alleluia, alleluia—sharing with Christ in his glorious Resurrection."

Visit, next, the most fearful of all graves, your own place of burial. See your name written on the stone marker and ponder that here your body has been buried to await your share in the Promise. Standing in front of your tomb, renew your belief in the promise that nothing can separate you from the love of Christ—not even death.

Pray for a happy death, at peace and reconciled with all. Pray that you will breathe your last still carrying your cross in a creative way that redeems you and the world. Pray for a happy death in which you will close your eyes totally attached to God, to Christ and his dream. Pray for a happy death, that you will die as a passionate lover, madly in love with life, with God and with all those whom you have cared for in the pilgrimage of this existence.

This seventh day was for the men and women disciples of Jesus the bleakest day of their lives. They awakened, shaken from their sleep by the impact of the death of their beloved master. They must have hoped that it all had been a nightmare. It had indeed been a nightmare, but a flesh and blood one. In agony they saw their beloved master die and with him their dreams for a new Israel. The promise that in their midst would appear the Reign of God in all its glorious justice was hung defeated and dead on a broken tree on the ugly hill of skulls.

To them, the next day, the first day of a new week, held nothing other than perhaps the promise of arrest and their own deaths. In fear and despair, they hid themselves. Today could be called Hiding Saturday. While empty, it was for them full of fears, doubts and questions.

Pray today for all who hide in fear at losing their lives because they have been part of a group which supported the liberation of the oppressed and the coming of justice to the poor and weak.

Pray on this last day of Holy Week for all who live in hopelessness, whose hearts hold no promise, no dreams. Their names are legion, the lost and forsaken who have given up the hope placed in inspired leaders, now dead.

Pray on this Holy Hiding Saturday for all those who hide out from life, from God, because they fear that life will require of them what was asked of Jesus of Galilee.

❀ ❀ ❀

Finally, having prayerfully traveled the forty days in the complicated passageways of the Lenten labyrinth, having strived to reform your life, it is time now to lay aside your sackcloth garment. Tonight is the most famous of all Saturday night baths. Treat yourself to a sacramental cleansing rite to symbolize the waters of new birth, the rising up of a new person.

Holding tightly to the Promise, conclude your vigil at the stone of the tomb of Christ. In your heart, light the lamps of hope and joy as you prepare for the greatest of all dawns, the most wondrous of all sunrises, Easter Sunday morning. As it has for two millenniums, that sacred sunrise will sing out in alleluia joy across the whole world announcing the good news of the glorious victory over the earthen family's archenemies, death and evil, announcing the first day of a new era and a new creation.

❀   ❀   ❀

EASTER SUNDAY
The Resurrection of Our Lord Jesus Christ

Easter's sunrise is a golden rose, the rose in the center of the labyrinth. Rejoice because you are standing in the center of that rose! John's account of the Resurrection of Jesus begins, "Early in the morning on the first day of the week..." (Jn. 20: 1). Mary Magdalene came to the tomb only to find it empty—yet filled with hope! She encountered the Risen Christ whom she mistook for the gardener. Christ then sent her off with a sunrise gospel, the good news: "Go to my brothers and tell them I am ascending to my Father and your Father, to my God and your God!" (Jn. 20: 17).

As Mary ran through the streets of Jerusalem to the hideout of the disciples, what do you suppose she was wearing? That may sound like a strange question, but what to wear on this Easter Sunday is perhaps the most common question of this morning. In Irving Berlin's famous Easter song, you are encouraged to:

Put on your Easter Bonnet with all the frills upon it.
You'll be the grandest lady in the Easter parade.

As the Risen Christ sent the apostle Mary Magdalene—she's entitled to be honored with that title since in Greek *apostolos* comes from *apostellein*, meaning "to send forth"—to proclaim the good news of the Resurrection message, was Mary wearing her Easter bonnet? If so, the frills on it were surely flying in the wind as she made her early morning dash through the streets of Jerusalem. After hearing the report, Peter and John hurried to the tomb. Were they wearing their Easter bonnets? It's not inappropriate, you know, for a man to wear a bonnet, even one which has ribbons on it. In Scotland bonnets are called tams; in France, berets.

These questions about clothing and headwear have a purpose—the tradition of Easter bonnets and new Easter clothes holds many insights into the Pascal Mystery. New clothing on this feast is directly connected to the Easter Sacrament of Baptism. Newly baptized adults originally were given white robes which they wore throughout Easter week. This custom soon expanded so that all Christians began to wear new clothes on Easter.

Newness fits Easter like a glove. The Easter ritual calls for new candles, new altar breads, new fire, new water to be blessed—all is to be new on this great feast. This mother of all Sundays and all holy days has about her a pungent perfume of newness; the feast is as new as the rising sun. So I hope you are wearing something new today.

There's an old Irish saying, "If you don't wear something new on Easter—and you can afford it—then bad luck will come upon you." The Irish also say that Christmas is about good food, drink and presents, and Easter is about new clothes. Well into the nineteenth century in England, it was believed that if you didn't wear something new on Easter you'd have a whole year of bad luck! It was also the common lore that if you failed to wear something new on Easter the dogs would spit at you. In America in the post Civil War days, nannies would tell their children, "If you don't wear something new on Easter—even new drawers—the crows will peck your eyes out, and when you go to church the birds will dirty you." The wearing of something new, then, was more than a matter of being in style; it was necessary for protection!

New clothing on Easter led to another important tradition of Easter:

> *I'll be all in clover and when they look you over*
> *I'll be the proudest fellah in the Easter parade.*

The parade in Berlin's song was once upon a time an important part of the celebration of Easter. Originally it began as an Easter walk, probably owing its roots to the familiar old expression, "All dressed up and nowhere to go." Those who kept the custom of new clothing on Easter went walking after church not for their health, but to show off their new attire to family and friends. Gradually the Easter walk grew into a real parade. The crowds in their Easter finery were joined by bands playing joyful music, by jesters and clowns. But all that was long ago, in the good old days, before the reformers came and proclaimed, "No parading on Sunday, especially on Easter Sunday!" Sober, stern reformers did indeed "rain on the parade," banishing, at the same time, Easter laughter.

On the Avenue, Fifth Avenue...

Berlin's song reminds us of a New York City relic of

that once jubilant, circus-like parade. Today's Easter parades still have the name but lack the color and excitement. Even if sometimes sporting a larger-than-life Easter Rabbit, the modern parade is more a stylish stroll. From the intensity of John's Resurrection Gospel story, I would wager that Mary Magdalene didn't stroll out of that cemetery garden with the radical good news entrusted to her by the Risen Christ. I imagine her bursting out in a sprint!

As she was personally commissioned by Christ Risen, so is every disciple sent forth with the good news of the victory of life over death. Irving Berlin's song implies that message in the line,

I could write a sonnet about your Easter bonnet.

Indeed, there's room to write a sonnet—or even a thesis—on the subject.

Like any lengthy consideration, an Easter sonnet or thesis would have plenty of questions to address. To begin with, a person, especially a person who doubts the reality of life after death, might ask the question, "Did Mary *bonnet* the disciples?" The expression "to bonnet" someone refers to the use of an underhanded accomplice to commit robbery at an auction, at the market or while gambling. Potential victims would be hoodwinked by having their cap or bonnet pulled down over their eyes. Did Mary hoodwink the apostles by saying that she had actually spoken with the Risen Messiah? Was it just a vision of her beloved master that she saw, the fantasy of one who wanted to believe he wasn't dead?

A second possible question in our Easter sonnet: "Was Mary Magdalene wearing what the French call a *bonnet rouge*, a red cap?" The red cap of liberty was worn by the conspirators in the French Revolution of 1789. Her Easter bonnet could have been red, not to match the red dress in which artists have frequently shown her as a sign of her former profession, but as a sign of her discipleship in the Easter Sunday Revolution which overthrew Dictator Death. Red, white and blue bonnets would be perfect for Easter since, like the Fourth of July, it celebrates freedom and liberty from the domination of death.

Those proclaiming, as did Mary, that the dead have risen from the graves might be accused of "throwing their bonnets over the windmill." It's an expression akin to throwing caution to the winds. If you believe that God raised Jesus up out of death and decay, you are throwing your bonnet over the rainbow as well. Somewhere over the rainbow, you can dance on the grave of the devil, on the grave of death itself.

Or it could be said that Mary Magdalene put a "green bonnet" over death. In seventeenth century France people who went bankrupt had to wear green berets. It's a wonderful Easter joke: Old Skeleton Death with a green bonnet on to symbolize that Death is bankrupt, out of business, since Christ has risen from the grave. Imagine if on this Easter Sunday, a boney skeleton wearing a green bonnet were to be placed on top of every old rugged cross which had been set outside a church during Holy Week. The solemn custom for the churches that use such crosses in Lent is to change the color of the cloth that drapes the cross on Easter Sunday from purple to white. Think of the laughter (and outrage) that a recycled Halloween green-bonneted skeleton dancing atop the cross would provoke!

Easter Sunday morning—once enlivened by band music, jesters and pealing bells, also rang out with *risus*

Paschalis, "Easter laughter." Long ago, after the forty long days of fasting and penance, after a Holy Week heavy with death-long worship services, cathedrals and parish churches were filled with *risus Paschalis.* Easter laughter, loud and wholesome, filled churches as priests made merry and told jokes. But that was once upon a time, before the Reformation. The sober, protesting reformers banished silliness from church, and the Catholic Church followed their example and, with tight upper lips, banished fun and folly from church.

If you're not wearing something new this morning on your way to church, I'd watch out for the dogs and birds! If you lack something new to wear, woe to you since you can look forward to 365 days of bad luck. Before you despair, however, take heart; there are solutions to your Easter problem. Consider how monks and nuns, religious men and women, must have felt about Easter's Nothing-New-Taboo, since they wore the same religious habit every day? On Easter, did the birds dirty them or the dogs spit at them?

On this Easter Sunday, and all the fifty days of Eastertide, you also can wear a habit—and not just one, but many new habits. Earnie Larsen in his book *Who's Driving the Bus—Co-dependent Business Behaviors of Workaholics, Perfectionists, Martyrs, Tap Dancers, Caretakers & People Pleasers* states that nearly 98% of what we do is habit! That can be good news, however, since not all habits are bad! During these forty days of Lenten prayer and reform, you surely have acquired a few new good habits. Wear those habits today.

Break, on this Sunday, with the old tradition of performing Lenten disciplines and prayer as a penance, only to return to your old habits as soon as Lent is over. This Easter, decide to continue those new practices. Let them make living a new life easier since habits are the source of 98% of your behavior. As new Easter attire, you can dress up in style by first wearing a new-heart habit. In these recent days of reform, you've struggled to form a habit of a new heart. Instead of your old-heart habits of clutching to resentment, grasping onto old gray-haired grudges and acid bitterness, you can practice good habits of pardon and reconciliation.

You learned habits of prayer, spiritual reading, taking time to nourish your soul, sharing your material gifts with those who are less fortunate than yourself. You practiced these and many other good habits of the spirit, so wear them proudly in the Easter parade. As the first Easter Sunday gave birth to new dreams for the first disciples, so this Easter can inspire you. Slip into a new habit of nursing dreams so wild that you have to "throw your bonnet over the rainbow" to chase after them. Wear, today and every day for the rest of your life, the habit of creating new dreams about your work, your love relationships and your way to God. Just as it's bad luck to wear old clothing today, it's also bad luck to not try on any new dreams. People without new or renewed dreams are dead, regardless of how young they are.

Put on your Easter habit of new loves. It's also bad luck, today and all 365 days of the year, to love *only* the same people you loved last Easter! Easter is the victory feast that is the fulfillment of the hard work which culminated in Good Friday when Christ died for everybody. During the days of this past Lent, you attempted to form the habit of loving others regardless of their religious beliefs or lack of them. You formed the habit of loving concern for aliens, for those whose skin is a different color, for those whose gender, sexual orientation or social status is other than yours. This morning, wear those beautiful heart habits to the parade.

As you walked the complex puzzle of the Lenten labyrinth, you formed the new habit of viewing life not as a series of problems but as an adventure. Whenever stopped by blank walls and dead ends in the maze, you acquired the *amazing*-grace habit of seeing responses other than weeping at your misfortune. Wear with Easter joy, not only today but the rest of your life, the new angles of vision, the new insights and prayerful exercises you acquired this Lent. Over all of these habits wear the habit of being a *pilgrim* on the journey through the great labyrinth of life.

This Sunday, if you've got a new Easter bonnet, wear it. If you have a dress, a new tie or a complete outfit of new habits, wear them as you join the Easter parade. Wear them today with the awareness that *someday*—which will arrive faster than you think—Old Boney Death is going to come and "bonnet" you! Death will pull his black wool cap over your eyes and you'll go to sleep. But fear not.

I solemnly assure you—I *solemnly* assure you—it will be only a very brief nap. Then, like Mary Magdalene, you'll hear Christ calling you by name. You will open your eyes with Christ singing:

> *Put on your Easter bonnet*
> *with all the frills upon it,*
> *and join in the great Easter parade,*
> *down Fifth Avenue*
> *and right through the gates of paradise.*